after the
MIRACLE

ILLUSIONS ALONG
THE PATH TO RESTORATION

DAVID B. HAMPTON

NASHVILLE

LONDON • NEW YORK • MELBOURNE • VANCOUVER

After the Miracle

© 2018 David B. Hampton

Published in New York, New York, by Morgan James Publishing. Morgan James is a trademark of Morgan James, LLC.
www.MorganJamesPublishing.com

The Morgan James Speakers Group can bring authors to your live event. For more information or to book an event visit The Morgan James Speakers Group at www.TheMorganJamesSpeakersGroup.com.

ISBN 978-1-68350-577-8 paperback
ISBN 978-1-68350-578-5 eBook
Library of Congress Control Number: 2017907269

Cover & Interior Design by:
Megan Whitney
Creative Ninja Designs
megan@creativeninjadesigns.com

In an effort to support local communities, raise awareness and funds, Morgan James Publishing donates a percentage of all book sales for the life of each book to Habitat for Humanity Peninsula and Greater Williamsburg.

Get involved today! Visit
www.MorganJamesBuilds.com

To those who are hiding in plain sight,
and the people who love them.

Contents

preface

Many of us would agree that we need a miracle in some area of our lives. But are we aware of how sick we really are? And are we aware that getting well comes with a price?

Why does the idea of getting healthy feel so threatening? Why did Jesus ask the paralyzed man by the pool if he wanted to be well instead of whether he merely wanted to walk again? What's the difference between being truly well and simply walking back home? And what was life like *after the miracle* for the man on the mat whose friends lowered their friend down to see Jesus and gave an unsuspecting host a new skylight?[1]

What are the tensions that come when we take up our mats and walk into a completely new life and way of being?

Why do so many marriages end during recovery rather than in the active addiction when things were supposedly so much worse?

Questions on top of questions. I have asked them and I suspect you have, too. *Which is why this book is for those of us who have looked up at life from our worn, crusty mats as well as those who have faithfully helped drag us along on them.*

We will never be so challenged as when we finally say *yes* to Jesus' question, "Do you want to be well?" We learn early on after the miracle of being restored to sanity that there is a surprising paradox in recovery, one that sends our expectations and the expectations of those around us clashing as we attempt to define our new normal. We realize that there are fresh tensions that present themselves as we assert our new and healthier way of being and believing with our loved ones who may not be quite ready for this different version of us. For many, we may be perceived as having become quite challenging. In other words, some people will like us better the way we were, back when we were sick, drinking, or acting out. After all, we have now formed actual opinions and are entertaining questions that never occurred to us during our sickness. Some of our loved ones may find this taxing. So now we find ourselves expressing fresh beliefs and old doubts, which we had neither the courage nor the initiative to articulate before.

At least in our sickness we were predictable, they might say.

Saying *yes* to God's invitation to wholeness is the beginning of the biggest adventure of our lives. After the miracle, we are often unprepared for what it will feel like to introduce our loved ones to a version of ourselves they have never met. Especially when the miracle was supposed to simply stop the leaking, kill the pain, heal the marriage, or fix the addict and *then* bring everyone back home to a business as usual life. Most of us would never entertain praying for the disruption that comes with becoming an entirely new individual, or even more scary, to wake up married to one.

Life will never be the same again after the miracle for anyone touched by it. It is easy to become frustrated by the idea that everyone may not celebrate the new version of us as much as we do. I believe this is why Jesus asks if we really want to be well instead of simply whether or not we want to get up and walk.

There are many realizations and realities to be reckoned with when we embrace what it truly means to be well. Maybe Jesus' words in "recovery vernacular" would sound more like, "Take up your reality and walk."

Or, "Take up your reality (cross) and follow me."

Everyone wants to walk, but not everyone wants to be well.

This book addresses the changes, challenges, tensions and triumphs that come with finally getting what we've prayed for.

Beware. This road is not for the faint hearted. It is a trip through the door that locks behind us as we find ourselves rolling up the mats that, for much of our lives, had once been our sickbeds. There is great joy and freedom ahead as God calls us out of our stuck places, but there are also untold challenges for which we must be prepared. My hope is that this conversation can help us prepare one another, as well as our fellow mat-carriers for what life beyond the miracle brings.

As a recovering alcoholic, a person who has lost a spouse to a long and grueling illness, and as a father who had to function as a single parent all while making a living as a "Professional Christian," I have experienced many versions of *the miracle*, not the least of which is my own sobriety. I have prayed, bargained with God, deceived myself as well as others, hidden, and done everything in my power to manage my own little world until I realized that it was I who was unmanageable. I practiced everything but surrender. What I experienced when God restored me to sanity was the surprise that very little of it came with the accolades I thought I would receive ... or frankly thought I deserved for making such a huge step. There was not much of a parade thrown for me by my closest loved ones after I answered "yes" to the invitation of wholeness. Instead, I was met with skepticism, indifference, and minimal encouragement by some of the closest people in my life, and in their defense, understandably so.

Why hadn't someone warned me that the miracle of my sobriety would require me to extend more patience to others as I invited them down this unfamiliar path with me?

It is my hope that we can not only take up our beds and walk, but that we can walk together as those who want to be whole. To do that we must be able to name the potential pitfalls of expectation and resentment we may experience when the people closest to us still aren't ready to throw congratulatory confetti in our honor. We have to remember that we have trained people how to treat us. Finding our voice can complicate their world as much as our own. We not only have to be able to name *our* pain, but be willing to allow others to name *theirs*. That is extremely challenging when the pain they identify has our name on it!

These dynamics and many others are the mile markers along the road to healing. *This book is meant to be a cautionary guide along the path and an inventory of the costs of shortcuts.*

Welcome to the view from down the road ... *after the miracle.*

Do you want to be well?

---

1   Matthew 9:1-8; Mark 2:1-12; Luke 5:18-26

chapter one
Dancing with Despair

All great spirituality is about what we do
with our pain. If we do not transform our pain,
we will transmit it to those around us.

RICHARD ROHR

I am learning that God is willing to show up and wait
for us in the strangest places when he wants to get our
attention.

Having successfully convinced myself once again that bad
judgment was my problem instead of alcohol, I was willing to
give the wheel another spin. Surely, I could drink like other
people if, this time, I applied myself and stuck to my two drinks

rule. Or maybe my drink-beer-and-wine-only rule. Then there was my drink-only-when-I-go-out rule. And I can't forget my only-drink-at-home-on-the-weekend rule. Name the scenario and I indiscriminately tried to embrace it in my futile attempt to believe I hadn't lost my power to choose after alcohol had been introduced into my situation.

On this particular morning, I woke up on the sofa and dragged myself down the hall to my bathroom. I felt the sting of fresh scabs on my knees and elbows. One look in the mirror revealed a man covered with bruises on his ribcage and forearms.

The unusual part was that I even looked in the mirror at all that morning. Most days I couldn't face my own reflection and I avoided mirrors like a vampire until well into the afternoon.

When I made my way back into the front of the house I noticed that there was toppled furniture and a broken dish in the kitchen floor. Near the broken dish was a shallow pool that I tried to convince myself to be the result of a leaky dishwasher or maybe an icemaker waterline that needed attention. As I crouched down to pick up the chipped dish I quickly realized that the puddle was my own urine.

This wasn't the first time I had come upon this little discovery.

Most of the time my morning-after episodes merely found me nauseated, tired from sleeping poorly, and struggling with extremely vague recollections of the night before (assuming I could muster any recollections at all). But this morning found me with injuries, something that had begun to happen with some regularity. As my head throbbed and my stomach soured from another previous night of excessive drinking and skipping dinner, I cleaned up the fallout of one more night gone wrong. Each chipped dish or toppled chair was like an exclamation point on the insanity that had become my life.

Drinking every day for the previous five years, and drinking heavily for more years before that was finally catching up with me. I reasoned that God must have a quota on the amount of alcohol any one human being can consume in a lifetime and I had apparently hit mine by the age of forty-five. When I wasn't waking up to this type of calamity I was waking up to some other type of alcohol related fallout. I had been known to try to crawl inside the wardrobe in our bedroom during the night or make phone calls that I couldn't recall. I was known to order delivery food and answer the door in my underwear with no memory of any of it. The boxes, food debris, and sacks in my bed were seldom enough to jog my feeble powers of recall. Yet, the evidence of stuffing myself while in one of my drunken stupors was pretty clear.

Arguments with my family were becoming more commonplace and I was told that despite the fact I was never physically abusive, I had said some very cruel and hurtful things. During one of my last drinking binges my wife Tricia and I had a bitter exchange after she confronted me about how much I was drinking. During the argument, I told Tricia—who by this time was suffering with a very stubborn and progressive form of MS—that if her life was such a living hell she could "divorce my sorry self and do us both a favor." After all, I wasn't exactly getting to enjoy all the bells and whistles of a conventional marriage anymore anyway.

The truth was that I was a walking case of caregiver burnout who carried a shot glass. I was tired of changing her adult diapers and giving her interferon injections. I was tired of having to catheterize her four times a day because she was unable do it herself. Juggling insurance statements, medical bills, scheduling home care, prescription orders, and acquiring the next necessary piece of medical equipment had become a job unto itself. I had to be trained in such unexpected specialties and for someone who "did music" for a living, I considered myself to be a barely adequate makeshift nurse.

It pained me to see my wife as a woman in her forties spending nearly all her time in bed or hobbling and falling as she tried to stay up on her walker. I was also more than done with accommodating her wheelchair when we went out everywhere. The sympathetic looks of the people who encountered us in the mall or in restaurants were glaring reminders that our lives were not like theirs. It didn't escape me that what most people shrouded in concern was, in reality, relief on their part that they were not us. Being a virtual single parent, breadwinner, professional Christian, nurse and caregiver was more than I had signed up for.

So, yes. Please divorce me so that we can both become someone else's problems.

On this regretful morning of overturned furniture, fresh scrapes, and bruised ribs I set out on the alcoholic's version of an Easter egg hunt. This is when I would shamefully and remorsefully wander through my house gathering up my hidden bottles from their secret storage places. Once I finally collected the loose bottles I placed them in an empty storage box, which I loaded into my SUV and made a pre-dawn run to the nearest dumpster.

This routine had become familiar. And, each time the committee in my head somehow convinced me that this would be the last time I would need to do this. Yet, as soon as the drop was made I would jump back into my vehicle and drive away with a gnawing sense of shame.

This day was no different.

We addicts are as addicted to our shame as we are our drugs of choice. Somewhere in our journey we got the idea that life required us to feel guilty, shameful, or "less than." We are defined by our secrets and grow so familiar with carrying shame around that we recreate opportunities to experience those feelings every chance we get. Our shame confuses self-condemnation with genuine repentance and mistakes self-loathing for appropriate contrition.

Upon returning home from my dumpster drops I tried to shower off the memories and wash away the previous night—another futile attempt to distance myself from the reality of what I had become. By noon I began to resemble a human being again and by four o'clock in the afternoon I began to think that my decision to stop drinking was a gross overreaction. By five I was considering ways to go back to the dumpster to reclaim my discarded supply. The despair and desperation that drove me to dispense of my wares would once again dissipate as I began to believe the lie that things could turn out differently next time.

And there was *always* a next time.

This was the dance of despair colliding with self-delusion. Once my despair gave way to rationalizing I was on my way back to redeem my bottles and give it another go.

When I returned to the dumpster that evening I noticed that there was an unusual amount of trash in the unit. My precious cargo was now buried at the bottom of a stinking mound of garbage the hot June weather had baked into a steaming, smoldering stench. Holding my breath, and still sore from my freshly bruised ribs courtesy of falling into the toppled furniture the previous evening, I hurled myself head first through the rectangular side opening of the trash container. Wading in waist deep, I tossed bag upon bag of garbage out of the way until I finally reached my box of discarded bottles. I hoisted the box out of the dumpster and carefully lowered it to the ground through the same side opening.

Before I could make my way out of the giant garbage pit, discernment came over me. The sensation was less like an out of body experience and more like hearing someone gently whisper in my ear. My deepest inner being distinctly experienced the words, "Look around you. You were made for so much more! Don't settle for this!"

The words rushed over me within only a matter of seconds, but they left an indelible impression on my heart. It was as if God had snapped a photograph of me and then handed it to me.

The pathetic part was that I didn't even recognize myself.

As I surveyed my surroundings I saw the extent of what I had become. Knee deep in garbage, hung over, alone, and wondering if I was just a little buzzed from breathing the vile funk of the dumpster, I suddenly recognized myself to be every bit the prodigal in the pigsty. The words in my head were *comforting*, but only to the extent that I could believe change was possible. But the words were also *confounding* because I simply didn't know how I was going to manage getting off this ride.

It would make a beautiful end to the story if I could say that I left my case of booze behind, jumped in my vehicle and sang "Amazing Grace" all the way home. Sadly, for those of us with addiction issues, the story rarely goes that way. Instead, I shook myself off, loaded the box into the back of my SUV and sped home to find new hiding places for my alcohol as well as myself. Shame tried to preach me its usual sermon from the passenger seat, but I was already plotting how I would drink again that evening. I rationalized that I probably had $100 worth of unconsumed liquor in that box and I wasn't about to *waste* it. I had convinced myself that this time I would certainly pace myself, use better judgment and make a point to be much more civil.

Of course, those promises soon waned along with the rest of my conviction as I got closer to home and to another night wrapped in the anesthesia of my liquid security blanket.

But, this time, I couldn't shake those few sentences that echoed in my head from the walls of the dumpster. Somehow, there was something inside me, a knowing that would nag at me with every glass. I would reach for a bottle and that voice would repeat itself. I would stagger to bed and those words would float to the top of my soggy brain. I didn't know how to reconcile myself with them. I finally decided that, if I couldn't stop on my own, it would be just like God to spike my drinks with conviction … which didn't endear me to him very much at the time.

I had grown so used to God's silence in my ambivalence that I found it a little ironic that he would just show up one day and drop these challenging declarations into my psyche from inside a trash heap. Why would he bother with interrupting my life when he never seemed to answer his phone when *I* called? Between asking him to heal my wife, strike me sober, and soften my daughter's heart toward me I was already reconciled to feeling as if I was getting his voicemail most of the time. After all, none of those things came to pass. At least not in the way I prayed for them. When was I going to get *my* miracle?

The snapshot from God that I experienced was like getting an invitation from him to the autopsy of my spiritual life. He was throwing back the sheets, leaving the ugly naked body in full view, every organ and fiber under extreme scrutiny and every rueful detail to be probed. I have since learned that he does these postmortems under the fluorescent lights of authenticity. I knew I was a spiritually bankrupt Professional Christian void of any real conviction, and numbed out from working in God's

Kool-Aid stand (also known as the church). Jesus was my *job*. Dishing up and selling the God Kool-Aid every weekend had taken its toll. Especially since I wasn't partaking. I just covered my shift. Not to mention that I found the stand itself to be a very dysfunctional place to make a living.

My growing desperation made it easier to consider seeking out a safe place in which to ask the questions I carried daily, and maybe even confess and say aloud the things that I had never told anyone. It would be some time later that I heard desperation referred to as a gift, a miracle that would lead me to the end of myself.

If I had known that it was going to be such a long trip I would have packed lighter.

So where does one go to admit that he or she is a high profile Professional Christian alcoholic? Where do you confess that you have written songs sung by people around the world that you aren't even sure you believe anymore? How does one face their most honest emotions when losing a spouse to a degenerative disease one bite at a time? Who is a safe person to tell that there are days that you *pray* for someone you love to die? Some days I would tell God that he could take either one of us. That I didn't care which one. Just put one of us out of this misery.

Who would help me understand that the disdain on my daughter's face for me was more than just teenaged angst? Where would I get the courage to admit that the public person I presented to the world didn't exist? How does one empty oneself of everything he thinks he knows about faith and start over?

And what if I don't believe what I thought I believed, or wish I believed when it is all said and done?

On some level I felt that I was ready to begin considering some of the hard facts about myself in God's autopsy report, at least the obvious ones. I could admit that *normal* people don't keep rum in the lawn spreader. I could concede that most Professional Christians don't make dumpster drops on their way to church. I was fairly certain most people didn't start their day in the bathroom the same way I did. I could even admit to the isolation that perpetuated my persona and the chasm between whom I *thought* I was and who I *really* was. What I couldn't do yet was say any of it aloud to another human being.

Was life just going to be a long journey of self-aware regret and remorse? Was my dumpster revelation something God was going to use to keep me perpetually discontent? Where would the help show up for me. And if it did, would I have the courage to take it by the horns and ride it into recovery? I knew deep down that this would be heart surgery of the most invasive order. Wondering what would be left of me when it was all over was more than I could even fathom contemplating.

So, I did the only thing I knew to do to quiet the voices that pelted me with reality and numb the pain. In the dusk of that summer evening I returned home, opened the hatch of my SUV and carried my little box of crazy back into the garage and shoved it under my wife's wheelchair ramp. I reached down into the box and grabbed a half-consumed handle of rum and took it into the house. The committee that lives in my head voted and told me I could make it work this time. It wasn't a unanimous vote but it was enough to convince me. I iced down a large patio tumbler, the same glass I had used every night for many years and poured. And thus, I embarked on the road to the end of myself, once again praying someone would stop me.

chapter two
End of the Road

The best way out is always through.
ROBERT FROST

My final drinking days were not so much a matter of coming to the end of the road as realizing that I had long ago blown through the "Dead End" signs. I had been driving on unpaved terrain for longer than I cared to admit and it had taken its toll on my family. My wife, who was in a wheelchair or bed most of the time by this time, had also been in her own fearful misery. She knew that her disease moved faster than she wanted to admit, its grim prognosis becoming undeniably progressive. She not only felt shackled by Multiple Sclerosis, she also felt like a prisoner of my addiction.

After enduring years of broken promises and my routine of "managed" daily drinking she came to some conclusions of her own. Divorce wasn't an option for her; she needed my health insurance. However, she also reasoned that she couldn't stand to stay with me any longer. She hatched a plan to keep our home as her legal address and live elsewhere and have her family help with her care. Our daughter Lauren was fifteen by this time and she had lost any grain of respect for me that she may have ever had. At home we came apart at the seams, while each week I put on a great show for Jesus doing the music he liked and trying to find ways to live with the reality of what I had become. No one in my outer circle knew my problem, and my inner circle didn't blame me for drinking given everything that they saw me trying to juggle. However, no one in the inner or outer circles knew the extent of trouble I lived in. I had persona management down to a fine art and, if everyone behaved, it went marvelously. The problem came as people were growing tired of their respective roles and didn't want to play anymore.

About a year before I completely hit the wall, my good friend, author and speaker Nate Larkin called to tell me about a test pilot for a new type of men's group he and some friends were going to start. He wanted me to be a part of the core group who would take the maiden voyage. They were calling it The Samson Society, named after the biblical character. Not because Samson was such a hero, but because Samson was the victim of his own isolation. Nate explained that whenever we see Samson in the Scriptures he was always going out alone. He had no band of brothers, no one to be honest with, and no one from whom he sought input. He was a man who believed his own press, which, in the end, had lethal consequences.

As a reminder to ourselves of the dangers of isolation the men had elected to call the group The Samson Society because, left to our own devices we are all natural born loners and liars. We eventually adopted the unofficial moniker of Pirate Monks. We decided that we were pirates at heart, prone to wander, fail miserably, and make reckless decisions. But at the core of our being we were monks with hearts for God despite our failures and shortcomings.

This group became a group built on confidentiality and trust. What is said, spoken, and even whispered in the sacred circle of those meetings is held in the strictest confidence. Every week we emphasize to newcomers that we are there to bear their burdens, deepest hurts, challenges, and mostly just to listen as we offer them a safe sanctuary in which to share their current reality for the week.

Today, The Samson Society has grown by multiple chapters across the United States and Canada. There is a Pirate Monks podcast and Nate has written an amazing book (*Samson and the Pirate Monks: Calling Men to Authentic Brotherhood*) highlighting his journey out of sexual addiction as well as how the birth of this group of men ultimately saved one another's lives. I'm honored to have been included in the formation of something that has been so life changing for so many.

In those early days, I attended the Monday night Pirate Monk meetings weekly as I listened quietly to men share their secrets, confess their transgressions, and wrestle with God. For the first several months we ironically met in the women's parlor at my church and the juxtaposition of tears, swearing, and men challenging one another juxtaposed with the backdrop of china cabinets, floral print pillows, and teacups with lace doilies was comical.

I had never encountered so many brave men who were willing to be that rigorously honest with one another. Every Monday evening I was like a scared grade-school boy at the deep end of a swimming pool. I wanted so badly to dive in to the water and bear my soul, my secrets, and my reality but my persona wouldn't let me. I was already good at giving the illusion of vulnerability so I went with that until I simply could no longer bear to sit with my feet dangling in the water, watching while the other kids had all the fun. It took a year of weekly meetings before I had the courage to finally tell someone what a day in the life of me looked like.

After a series of even more potentially serious consequences where my drinking was concerned, I finally had to reach out to someone. I called Nate and invited him to coffee. Nate had a story that I couldn't imagine having the courage to share and yet he did it with candor and joy. I knew that he was involved in 12-step recovery and even though I was sure I wouldn't need to do anything that drastic, I thought he might have some ideas about how I could learn to manage my drinking.

Nate also had a language that he spoke at our Monday night meetings unlike anything I was accustomed to hearing at church. The fresh implications of familiar words came across with a unique ring to them that I found intriguing and captivating. It was a language he learned at his other meetings, the meetings that gave him the vocabulary of recovery. His comments never sounded as if they came from a place of performance or as if he was trying to impress God with his piety. I decided that if Nate could share his reality with the masses, I could at least share mine with him.

After a few of those visits and a lot of coffee, I told Nate my story. I shared the consequences, the nature of my habits, how I had tried numerous times to stop myself, and the shame of my multiple failed attempts. What Nate already knew was that anytime someone precedes their comments with, "I think I might have a problem with..." they most likely do. Nate asked me if I had ever attended a 12-step recovery meeting for alcoholics. With all sincerity, I asked him why I would consider something like that. I wasn't an alcoholic. I just drank like one. I was, however fresh off another dumpster dive and was desperate enough to consider anything he suggested.

From there, on a hot summer day in June, Nate walked me across Main Street into the historic, civil war era Methodist church that would ultimately become another sacred space in my life. Nate carried my mat. He lowered me through the roof. He took me to get help and walked with me daily in those early days because he believed in the miracle that he himself experienced. He didn't just hand me a phone number or point me down the block to the picturesque red-brick church that held "the meetings." Instead, he took me. Eventually, there were more mat-bearers and more friends whose faith I would need to borrow.

I treasure every one of them.

I remember feeling such a sense of defeat as I took every stair step into that church basement. I felt as if I had gotten stranded at the rest stop for losers and people who couldn't take control of their lives. I looked around the room passing judgment on every single person in my gaze. Surely, I wasn't one of *those* people. I soon realized that they were exactly like me, and I indeed am one of *those* people. There were trial lawyers, soccer moms, mechanics, bankers, gay people, straight people, white, black and brown people, grandparents, homeless, and business professionals. Being in the Nashville area, there was also the sprinkling of people whose music I had enjoyed over the years or their roles on television and movies that were familiar to me, all sitting in a big circle on a level playing field of addiction. There was a common thread of desperation, gratitude, and joy in those rooms, as if everyone knew that this was their last stop and they were determined to do what had worked for thousands before them in order to enjoy what thousands before them had discovered. They had checked their uniqueness at the door and came in with open hands and hearts full of gratitude. No one was more special than anyone else, and yet we were all people who had made a life out of feeling special. In their sacred circle, there was the same freedom to be brutally honest and completely transparent just as I had experienced on Monday evenings with my Pirate Monk companions. Resentments were addressed specifically as if to gloss over them would have deadly consequences. Entitlement was called out for what it was and there was no sympathy for the victim mentality on this bus. The victim with a sense of entitlement was recognized as a very dangerous mindset to someone struggling with escapism and substances.

I did ninety of those meetings in ninety days (as well as hundreds more in the years to come). Nate suggested the importance of a sponsor; eventually I got someone to sponsor me. A recovery friend introduced me to a man I'll call Stewart. Stewart had no filter, or if he did he obviously hadn't changed it in a few decades. He was several years older than I and had his own devastating yet redemptive stories that he generously shared. Stewart had also built a very high profile career for himself but in politics so his B.S. meter was very finely tuned and in excellent working order. I began to understand that Stewart, like the many others in those rooms, found freedom in sharing where they had been, what happened to them, and who they are today. It reminded them that they didn't want to go back. It was part of their process to walk with people like me who couldn't imagine going ninety minutes without a drink, let alone ninety days, weeks, or months.

The first question Stewart ever asked me was if I wanted to be sober. I told him of course I did. I didn't *want* to drink anymore. It was ruining my life, my family, and I was unable to hide it any longer. Stewart quickly stopped me and said, "I'm not asking you if you want to stop drinking. I'm asking you if you want to be sober. There is a big difference. The world is full of dry drunks who aren't sober. I'm asking you if you're willing to submit yourself to examining your life in a way that you never have. I'm inviting you into a place of rigorous honesty and a community of people who will love you no matter what you've done, what you believe, or what you say. At the end of the day, if you want to be sober I can help you. If you just want to stop drinking, I can't.

"Sobriety is a new way of living, looking at yourself and others, learning what is true surrender, owning what is on your side of the street and turning yourself over to the care of God. And speaking of God, I don't want you giving me a bunch of churchy, crap. I'm a Christian and I'll smell you trying to put a church patch over this a mile off. This isn't about whether you believe a certain doctrine. Your position on baptism didn't keep you sober. This is about whether you want to meet God on his terms, not yours, and quit preaching to him and calling it prayer. Praying for his will to be done and the courage and wisdom to live in and with it is what this program is about. We don't tell God what to do here."

"We surrender, we recognize the reality of what we are, and accept others regardless of where they've been or what they believe. If you want to be a part of this kind of community, then I will walk with you daily. If you need to go out and do more research and decide if this is what you need I'm okay with that too. I'm sober today either way. This is completely up to whether you are at the end of yourself or not."

My head swam. In all my Christian experiences, no one had laid out a gut level picture of what it looks like to truly surrender like Stewart had laid out on me. It wasn't based in shame. It wasn't a set of guilty emotions or a list of "sins." It was simply holding up a mirror in one hand and hope in the other and calling out what we both saw.

That evening was the beginning of my new way of being, thinking, and understanding. I realized I truly wanted to be well, but it scared the hell out of me to even consider facing my life without anesthesia. What would happen to the bomb of anxiety that I carried strapped to my chest? Who or what would give me permission to diffuse that? What if I offend people with this rigorous honesty business Stewart kept referring to? How would church people perceive me when the reality of my doubts and questions came up, let alone when they find out where I am spending my lunch hour?

The miracle I began to experience that evening set in motion a process that, by God's grace, continues to this day. I said "yes" to wellness rather than to performing. I embraced the opportunity to borrow the faith and experience of others as I stepped out into the uncharted territory of letting people see behind my mask. The courage to allow anyone behind the curtain of my reality only came from observing the freedom of others who had experienced doing the same. I began to realize that I had been drinking at specific people and situations in my life, which needed to be surrendered. I had a list of emotional hostages that needed to be released. All these steps began my journey through the miracle of desperation and gratitude.

At least now it was *my* journey.

It would take months and years for some around me to buy in and suspend their suspicion of me let, alone celebrate me. My new sense of boundaries and realizations didn't exactly line up with how I had trained people to treat me. For some, after my miraculous collision with desperation and gratitude, I became rather challenging as a more authentic version of me began to emerge. And this is when I realized that it is when desperation and gratitude intersect that true worship happens.

We see it in the story of the leper who returns to Jesus and falls at his feet and worships him from a place of gratitude. Moments before he had simply been a desperate untouchable seeking a miracle. Suddenly, in an instant of clarity, he runs back and falls at Jesus' feet in an act of thanks and worship.

I believe it is significant that he had to go back down the road for a stretch before he realized the full extent of what had happened to him. Sometimes we need to have some distance between the miracle and ourselves to truly experience the depth of our gratitude.

As I think back about the man at the pool and Jesus' puzzling question, "Do you want to be well?" I realize I was learning the difference between simply wanting to walk and wanting to be whole. Simply wanting to walk is just performing, which I had done all my life. Wanting to be *well* means everything I thought I knew will now be seen through a new lens. *Wanting* to be well is saying yes to the challenges, the personal inspection, and the commitment to community that will keep us walking long after the miracle.

chapter three
The Monk at the Fork in the Road
—Part 1—

There are only two ways to live your life.
One is as though nothing is a miracle. The other
is as though everything is a miracle.

ALBERT EINSTEIN

T hose of us in recovery often hear the warning: *don't make any life-changing decisions or choices in the first year of sobriety.* I have begun to understand the wisdom in such advice after experiencing my own first year of sensory overload sans alcohol.

I was totally unprepared for the feeling of giving up the anesthesia I had been under for so long. After my first three or four days without alcohol, I realized why rehab centers exist in the first place. I can see now that the journey back into reality is one best embarked upon away from other people. It just doesn't seem fair to the rest of the world to have to put up with our reentry into society ... and all that goes with it.

Having shared that bit of hindsight, I must now admit that I elected not to enter rehab to sober up—despite my advice to the contrary. Maybe my strong Midwest work ethic convinced me I should have been able to tackle this outside of an expensive treatment facility. Maybe I totally underestimated the levels of angst, paranoia, panic, rage, and fear I would experience.

Maybe I was just stupid.

Nonetheless, I began my crossing into clear-headedness with ninety AA meetings in ninety days and by enlisting the help of a sponsor whom I called a couple of times a day those first several weeks. The meetings continue to be a part of my regular routine, and I have a number of people who I talk to on a very regular basis even today.

By electing to do my initial twelve-step work outside of treatment and inside the anonymity of recovery meetings, the rest of me was pretty much consumed with simply trying to stay in step with the rest of my life and continue working. Every day I dodged in and out of those noontime AA meetings in the basement of a local church as if I were sneaking in and out of a strip club. Getting caught coming and going from what everyone in town recognized as the noontime AA meeting would have been like having my picture snapped in an adult bookstore. It took some time for me to get over the self-imposed stigma. At some level in my deepest core, in the beginning I believed that those meetings represented failure and defeat. I remember sitting in the back of the room against the cinderblock walls in cold metal folding chairs, sunglasses hiding my empty, detached stare. At first, the thought running through my mind everyday was, "So, it's come to *this*?" It took some time before I began experiencing the joy about which I'd heard others in those rooms speak of. It took even longer before I realized that meetings didn't represent the end of the road for me—instead, they represented the beginning.

I reasoned that Tricia needed me at home and to go away for twenty-eight days was a terrible and unnecessary burden to place on my family. My daughter was only fifteen at the time, so I couldn't justify leaving her for a month with a mother who, by then, needed constant care. Lauren's resentment level toward me already soared off the charts, and I saw no need to throw gasoline into the furnace by announcing that I was going away for a month to get well. So, I began this journey the only way I knew how at the time, and God was gracious and merciful in allowing me to experience tiny pockets of sanity that eventually, when strung together, evolved into my sobriety.

By *no* means did I experience smooth sailing. In fact, I have a bookcase with a missing pane of glass in one door, and my office walls suffered a couple of deep gashes where I threw a stool a few times. Since those tumultuous early days, I have painted the walls of the office, and those scars were easily spackled over. But my other scars didn't disappear quite as easily. Depending on the day, I had bouts of complete depression and bouts of utter rage. I saw both what my life had been and what my life might look like in the future—and neither option looked terribly glamorous. The only thing I could do was not drink, go to meetings, not drink, call my sponsor, not drink, and stay home and not drink.

The best way I can describe coming out from under years of constantly numbing myself into oblivion on a daily basis (and yes, I drank daily for at least my last five years at it) is that every one of my senses was on "stun" once I stopped. My state of awareness turned up to eleven, and I found no escape from all the stimuli that felt about three inches from my face every second of every day. I was as nervous as a circus poodle and I couldn't get away from myself. The sheer sensory overload was like nothing else I have experienced in my life.

A big part of my justification for drinking was so I could handle my feelings of anxiety. Ironically, without alcohol I was nothing but anxious and had no tools with which to cope ... or so I thought. I remember wondering, "When did everything get so irritatingly *loud*?" A phone ringing sent me through the ceiling. I treated even the simplest of interruptions like the Spanish Inquisition. One unexpected challenge or encounter received ten times its deserved response. Minute by minute, I had to learn to adjust to these stimuli as I started leveling out during the weeks that followed. It took a while, but my body finally accepted that I meant business with this self-imposed prohibition.

Here's the bigger story: everything I had stuffed emotionally, spiritually, and relationally over all those glorious drinking years (and the first several years really were glorious) jumped out at me like a jack-in-the-box. Relationships had become a virtual minefield. No one was accustomed to "the new me," and I certainly wasn't used to dealing with them without a little help from my friend. Suddenly I had opinions. All of a sudden I seemed contentious to my family, friends, and colleagues—and truthfully, I probably was. The new place in which I lived inside myself demanded immediate answers to everything.

I wondered when it became okay for people to speak to me in certain ways. I wondered when it became acceptable for me to allow certain people to shame me or take advantage of me.

In their defense, I had trained them in the way I thought I deserved to be treated, and they obliged. I didn't want to be bothered with decisions in the height of my addiction, so they made decisions for me. I didn't want to take responsibility for things, so they took them. I didn't want to be intruded upon when I was medicating, so I trained the world to march around me, and even to enable me. Then I woke up, got sober, and expected the game to come back to me overnight. The people in that close inner circle of mine looked at me with a bit of disbelief.

And frankly, with disdain. They had run this show for a while without me, and I decided to go and get sober on them, plowing up their playing field in the process.

The whole part of the spiritual equation turns into a complete melt down for many of us who thought we knew what we believed, especially those of us who come from certain evangelical circles of faith, particularly fundamentalism. I don't necessarily consider myself evangelical, and I'm certainly not a fundamentalist. But suddenly, I didn't know anything that I thought I once knew or believed to be true about God, my spiritual self, or where Jesus had been hanging out while I had been drinking my butt off.

The huge cornerstone of recovery is establishing or reestablishing what the steps refer to as "your center of faith in a Higher Power" or "a God of our understanding." I realize this is where many good and well-meaning Christians get nervous. It sounds as if we get to create God in our image, name him George, and wave at him while he trims his hedges in flannel pajamas—or something to that effect. That isn't necessarily the case. I can only speak from my experience, but I had to take virtually everything I thought I knew about God, faith, and redemption, put it on a shelf, and add it back a little at a time.

Some things never fit the same way again, and I had to lose them. Some things are even more precious to me now than they were before. Either way, these things had to be confronted, because I, like most of us in recovery, felt like I had dropped off God's radar, and he never bothered to send out a search party.

At least that is the argument that my victim voice on the committee likes to make.

Professionals who deal with drug and alcohol abuse patients will concur that Christians are the hardest people in the world to get sober because we come in thinking we know all the answers when it comes to concepts like "surrender," the role God plays in our daily lives, and "victory" over life's obstacles. As addicts, we are spiritually bankrupt. Still, somewhere in the deepest part of our addiction, we cling to old answers, practices, and notions, lest we negate our traditional way of faith—which is probably what needed to happen in the first place, after all.

My somewhat schizophrenic mind used to conjure up inner dialogues like this:

"Isn't this addiction thing just a matter of deep sin and sincere repentance anyway?"

"Maybe if I had been sincerer in my last repentant prayer from the toilet at six a.m., I'd be able to shake this thing. I'll try harder to be sincerer."

"I'll make more promises and mean them this time."

"Maybe God will take this from me if he knows how truly sorry I am–again."

"I believe in healing. I believe in a God who wouldn't let me go through this misery. Why is this continuing, and why can't I stop if God only wants what is best for me?"

"I don't want recovery. I want a miracle! I believe in miracles!"

"Why is God being so silent? Is my life just a cosmic joke?"

"When did I lose the power to choose? If I can do all things through Christ who strengthens me, why am I powerless over something like this?"

"These recovery people insist that I admit powerlessness as a first step. That is antithetical to my beliefs. I am *not* powerless! I'm *not* an alcoholic—I just can't stop drinking!"

As good Christian people, we have been groomed to "know" things. We are supposed to have answers to support our faith and we should be able to give an account to show ourselves approved unto God.

Or something to that effect.

Nonetheless, when I wake up at 2:00 in the morning with pizza boxes in the bed and I don't remember ordering a pizza, paying for a pizza, or eating a pizza, I am pretty much fresh out of those highly esteemed spiritual insights. Answers and knowledge (or the lack of it) was never my problem. "Should" and "ought" weren't the most helpful words to me at that point, either. These words only served to channel the shame already looming over me like a ghost. I didn't understand why "should" wasn't enough to keep me out of this crazy-making behavior I created. Those words, "should" and "ought" certainly hadn't kept me sober and certainly hadn't kept me from being flagged in the Domino's Pizza system as an "interesting" customer.

About eight months into my sobriety, I decided that if I was going to be able to continue in any kind of faith system (let alone make my living working within one) I would have to go away to do it. Ironically, I tackled the onset of the alcohol portion of my recovery with help at home, but to make any spiritual headway in my journey I decided I would have to get out of Dodge and go see the rest of Kansas. I found myself at a pivotal spiritual and emotional fork in the road. I had lost confidence in my own personal Christian traditions and needed to hear fresh words from fresh people in a fresh place.

A couple of my close friends had been to a monastery in southern Indiana, not far from my hometown. They told me of their experiences with something they called "guided retreats." The term "guided" honestly made me uneasy because I wasn't one to be led around. Still, at this point I decided that a guide along the path might be in order.

And if the guide had a lantern, he'd better bring it—because where I walked was very dark.

chapter four
The Monk at the Fork in the Road
—Part 2—

Miracles are a retelling in small letters of the very same story which is written across the whole world in letters too large for some of us to see.

C.S. LEWIS

One friend told me that being at the guided retreat had been unlike any experience he'd ever experienced. The happenings he recounted to me were those of transcendence, exercises in silence, and lovingly skillful leadership walking him through aspects of his story that may have gotten overlooked or at least glossed over in his own personal inventory. Most of all, for my friend, this time away marked the beginning of a new way of thinking about prayer, encountering God, peace, grace, and what it meant to see God as a living and breathing part of his life.

Between the challenges that the recovery process brought to my narrow spiritual perspectives and the fact that I even considered going up and hanging out with the monks of St. Meinrad for a few days, I feared that I might have indeed completely lost what I thought was left of my mind.

On my own, I couldn't get to the root of why I was so out of sorts about the things I made a living trying to encourage people to believe. Questions in general were something I wasn't completely comfortable with. As the Professional Christian, I learned long ago to keep my questions to myself. I hadn't been to seminary and I'm not a theologian. I'm a very fortunate piano player who became a songwriter who ended up in a great job with people I love dearly. And I sure didn't want to screw it up doing my impersonation of Doubting Thomas all over everyone.

Over the years of my Christian experience, I found myself in that no-man's land of having to take the word of the scholars for my spiritual peace of mind and check my doubts at the door. The roles of the "scholars" changed as my various denominational bents changed, and each set of "scholars" had their own take on "truth." Settling for stock answers and official denominational positions on the issues of my life wasn't cutting it for me as a person who had begun to think soberly. It had worked for the *drinking* version of me, but the emerging sober version wasn't having any part of it.

I remember sitting in staff meetings that first year and hearing certain spiritual perspectives as if for the first time ... and not necessarily always in a good way. Things made a bell go off in my head like an egg timer signaling that the egg was cooked. I could feel one eyebrow raising and my head snapping to one side like Scooby-doo's when he hears something suspicious. It was like the cliché sound of the needle dragging across a revolving record while the room stood still in my mind. I wanted to say things like, "I don't think what I heard you say makes any sense." Or: "What? I don't think I believe that. When did we start professing that? When did that issue become a deal breaker?" And: "I hope I don't have to buy that to be a Christian because I think that's a load of crap!"

Thankfully, whatever modicum of good judgment I had maintained prevailed and those questions stayed within the repository of my somewhat soggy but slowly reawakening brain.

All I really knew was that my boat leaked badly, so I decided to make my reservations at the monastery and take my chances with the monks. My wife's parents were willing to take care of things at home with Tricia, and Lauren was finally able to deal with the idea of my being out for short stretches of time, so I went for it. So, I took some time off using vague and illusive excuses, then made my way up to Indiana for several days.

Upon arriving at the St. Meinrad Monastery in the small town of St. Meinrad, Indiana, I decided to keep a journal. It seemed like a good idea for me to have some type of archive to look back on one day. I had begun to discover things in my life that I might *want* to remember, and I thought this trip might be one of those things.

I wasn't at the monastery long before I realized I was going to have plenty to journal about. These Catholics are hardcore, and their practices aren't for sissies. I quickly learned that if I was there to confront my inner "stuff" seriously, then I would have every opportunity to turn over every rock that had settled into the hard, dry sod of my heart and soul. But, if I was just there to have my ego stroked and get my picture taken with a monk, then I should have saved my money.

My "guide" (or "spiritual director," if you will) was a monk named Father Bennett. A quiet and thoughtful man, he seemed to take an unusual amount of time formulating his thoughts before making a reply. He had a very dry, edgy sense of humor as well. I hadn't expected such a sense of humor from a monk, which attracted me to him right away.

Example: when he found out that I was employed by a Presbyterian church, he said, "Oh, man. You must really be screwed up if the Presbyterians approved your coming up and letting the Catholics get a hold of you!" He laughed in a self-amused way and then settled back in to the gravity of our conversation.

I expected somber and solemn demeanors and found just the opposite among the brothers at St. Meinrad. Peaceful but unmistakable joy manifested itself in nearly every encounter I had in that place.

The excerpts (below) from my retreat journal cover about a four-day period. These are by no means every entry I wrote, nor are they the most personal. But, they are here to offer a peek into where I was coming from at the time and to show the raw and fragile condition of my reawakening heart.

My sponsor back home had been stressing to me that sobriety wasn't just the state of not drinking. Instead, sobriety was a mindset, a lifestyle, and a new way of dealing with life in a whole different paradigm. To do that, I needed a spiritual base that supported my new way of being. My new way of being began here, at St. Meinrad's—the place where living soberly took on new meaning for me.

From my journal, raw—exactly as I wrote it:

As I arrived at the abbey it was as if I had driven up a main road in southern Indiana, taken a right turn and ended up in Europe. One minute I'm in the cornfields of the Indiana countryside and the next minute it is as if I've been beamed to the lush green hillsides of Switzerland. The abbey is beautiful with the rich, gothic look of its European heritage and symbols that we don't see much in Protestant culture. The monks walk about the grounds and farmlands in their traditional hooded robes (habits) and process into the church single file for early morning prayers and vespers. Prayers start at 5:30 a.m. I'm taking that to mean that God clocks in early around here. Needless to say, I missed that this morning. I'm getting the impression that time is a pretty strict thing around here as well. Bells chime from the steeples on the hour and half hour (even one chime every fifteen minutes), and people are very careful to tell you exactly when things begin and end. They are obviously very Swiss/German in their heritage, manner and culture.

I have been assigned a "spiritual guide" here. His name is Father Bennett. He is an interesting sort of guy. He's very much a thinker and seems to ponder every word. He has asked me what I want from this retreat and my time with him. That is actually an interesting question. He wants me to list some things I'd like to cover and then we'll "go with it," he says.

For all the time I spent anticipating this trip, about the only thing that I can say I want to come away with is peace and clarity: Clarity of who God is and who I am. His will for my life and how to know that. I want to learn to listen to God speaking to me (assuming he does). I want to have my image of God healed, my notions of what I really believe cleared up, and the freedom to live by that. I want to be a "real" Christian but I don't know what that is anymore. I know how to be a professional one. You just do your job, keep your questions to yourself, and don't tip your hand. You give people their big spiritual orgasm every week, and if you know how to do that well then you live to fight another day. That isn't what I want for the rest of my life.

I told him that I was honestly very confounded by the idea of prayer and that I really had only begun to pray again recently since entering recovery. He asked me why I thought that was and I told him that I was fairly sure that I was either doing it wrong, praying for the wrong things, praying with bad theology, or just praying outside the will of God so the perfectionist in me voted and decided that we just didn't really need to engage in it anymore. Besides all that, after my wife's rapidly declining health, it feels very futile. I don't pray for safe trips anymore. I don't pray for health. I don't pray for personal prayer requests that people email me. I'm not going to change God's mind and the most I can think to pray for, assuming I would, is peace, courage, and wisdom because those are the only things I know God promises for sure.

I'm looking forward to my time with Father Bennett again this evening. I have lists to make, and he wants me to pray while I make them. That is going to be an interesting exercise. He says most people never learn to listen to God and that is the other half of prayer. Prayer isn't just the drive-by "throwing our needs out the window at God" and moving on. It isn't treating him like the drive-thru window at Burger King. It is letting our cares be heard and then being silent. Father Bennett says that we evangelicals like to preach at God in our prayers. He says that prayer is as much about letting God talk back to us. He says God speaks in scripture, situations, "coincidences," affirming words from people, stirrings in our own hearts, our own unrest, disappointments, etc. He feels that perhaps we just learn to call it different things and never perceive it as God speaking to us. He says prayer is a discipline, not just a mere ritual. It takes time to learn to pray and time to learn to listen, and it takes quiet.

Pretty much answers why my prayer life sucks.

I'm looking forward to tonight's time and more insights from him.

After my list-making assignment and my "prayerful" personal assessment of what I really wanted God to bring to bear in my life, I met with Father Bennett again. The following entry was written after that meeting.

I met with Father Bennett again this evening. I brought in my exhaustive list of things I wanted cleared up before I leave and he read it, smiled and handed it back to me. He told me that the answers I'm looking for are already in front of me and I needed to spend time reflecting. Meditate on things that I have been reading and see what those things are telling me. Are there similarities with my conversations with others? He proposed that sometimes God allows those to be part of the realization process for us that awaken us to our own desperation.

Near the end of our hour he made another point that has really stuck with me. He kind of tied together these things that I thought were just fragments of unrelated, frustrating pieces in my scattered spiritual puzzle. He pointed out that my desire to hear God and listen would result in challenging my prayer life. He said that it is a lifetime of learning, but it becomes clearer as we are disciplined to do it—something that I never thought about.

Father Bennett went on to make this point: "You are at a place in your life where you admit that there are only a couple of things that you believe in—the sovereignty of God and the finishing work of Jesus, and from there you are pretty wide open. Why don't you let God reinvent you? Let him talk to you. Let him tell you that some of the 'blanks' that you have are okay. Embrace the fact that he's passionate about you. Relax in not having to be so 'right' and learn to let God speak to you and just speak to him honestly. It may surprise you. You have a beautiful, blank canvas in front of you and you need to be empowered to take it on."

I felt as if I could weep. I haven't felt empowered or free to open myself up to the person God would have me be. I have been in this paralyzed place for so long: My wife's illness, my illness, my fear, my persona, my shortcomings as a parent and my diminishing faith in faith have all worked like a well-oiled machine to render me numb and detached. I have buried myself in isolation and self-protection and then find myself wondering why God isn't coming through.

I have such a sense of why I am where I am now. It is part of the human endeavor to make mistakes and let God teach us through our own frailty, even sin. I actually feel like maybe I'm on to something here. It is as though there is room in God's economy for my doubts and my questions.

Maybe my frustrations and fears don't frustrate him at all.

Over the next few days, I spent a great deal of my time with Father Bennett and presented him with some tough questions. I grilled him about life, God, heaven, hell, suffering, addiction, raising children, peace, God's will, how to listen to God, how reading the Bible can be more confounding than comforting, the duality of my persona as a professional Christian vs. the "real" me, and how I think like a victim in any and all of it. Not too much to ask one Benedictine monk in a few days' time. Since I had about four days blocked out for this time, I planned to give every second of them a run for my money! After all, what did Father Bennett really have to do but listen to me anyway—I mean, other than to sit around praying and maybe dish up soup?

One of the things challenging my views of God at that time was how God works in the lives of all people (and the world) and at times how he seems almost to do what he does despite the Church rather than through it. Not only does this confuse me— it's bad for business if you're employed in a vocation like mine and want to believe that the Church really makes a big dent in the world for Jesus. I approached the subject of God working within and without the Church with Father Bennett. The monk thought for a minute, rubbed his head as seemed to be his customary precursor to profundity, took off his wire framed glasses, and then said, "We cannot say precisely what God is doing or how God chooses to reveal himself, or to whom. God can use an atheist to speak truth if he wants to, even if the atheist isn't aware of it. Furthermore, these people in your recovery groups *are* experiencing God. They aren't from your tradition or my tradition. They are coming from a place of emptiness and God is meeting them there. Who knows how he will show himself. Just because they haven't been baptized in your church or mine doesn't mean that they aren't experiencing God's truth or that they are somehow ultimately misguided."

That said, he really started to rattle my cage.

chapter five
The Monk at the Fork in the Road
—Part 3—

*The difference between you and God is that
God doesn't think He's you.*
ANNE LAMOTT

*G*od has used many great people in the world," Father Bennett continued, "who may not fit your grid or mine when it comes to how they define themselves in his kingdom. Yet, they have devoted their entire lives to doing justice, loving mercy, and walking humbly with him.

"You'll find that I'm not one of those guys who thinks Gandhi is in hell, by the way. You can't tell me that the selfless life that he lived trying to bring attention to the downtrodden in his culture was simply an exercise in futility and that it wasn't a gift from God that he felt both compelled to do it and had the grace to carry it out. All that, I believe, came from God. I believe Gandhi knew Jesus. Gandhi is in heaven as far as I'm concerned.

"Now, does that mean that you and I can go off and join the Hari Krishna's? I don't think so, and here's why: I'm saying that you and I have been given the gift of knowing Jesus here and now. The Way, the Truth, and the Life. I've known people from Christian traditions who have gone off and joined eastern religions thinking that will solve their disillusionment with the Church universal. It doesn't. It is like watching someone trying to wear a suit of clothes meant for someone else. It just looks ridiculous on them and they don't really wear it well because they really know better in the core of their souls. You know the Truth and can't claim ignorance now. They, in these other places and cultures may not.

"So, when someone in AA doesn't know 'truth' by our definition but is definitely experiencing life-changing miracles wrought by prayer and seeking God, even if it is 'the God of their own understanding' as they say, isn't that what we all do? I call that God's Common Grace and Mercy.

"None of us ultimately knows all there is about God, and even though the American church wouldn't like this, we have largely created a God of our own understanding in many churches and denominations today as well.

"No, I'd have to say that they are experiencing God and Jesus in a very genuine way, as are people around the world even if they don't call it that yet. God has revealed himself to everyone in some way and they all have a means of celebrating him. Jesus will reconcile these things to himself in the end."

In that moment, I paused and tried to take in what for me was a lot to digest. Suspended in some cosmic space with God, Father Bennett, and my thoughts for a timeless moment, my guide continued. "If you give someone a gift, the pleasure in giving it isn't just watching them open it and seeing their surprise. It is seeing that gift become useful to them. Seeing them share it. Seeing that gift make their lives richer. Seeing how that gift frees them up from something that was otherwise very difficult for them. Seeing the gift bring them joy.

"This is how I believe God feels about his gift of grace. It is a free gift that he bestows on us, but his real joy in giving it to us is when he sees us learn to embrace it and watching it change our lives. My challenge for you isn't whether or not you've experienced the miracle of God's grace. You have many times and not the least of which was when you embarked on sobriety. My challenge for you is whether or not you are willing to embrace the God who is enjoying watching you open this beautiful present and learn to use the tools that come with it."

Then he paused before adding, "Do you believe God loves you?"

I was blindsided. Of course I believe God loves me! I have been told that God loves me all my life. What kind of half-witted Monk 101 question was that? I was insulted he would think I hadn't moved from the pre-school level of Christian understanding as though I had never addressed that question. My answer was quick and a bit curt.

"Of course! I *know* God loves me." I did what I could to disguise the slight sting of irritability in my voice.

His eyes narrowed. He leaned in and said, "Do you *believe* that God loves you? I'm not asking you if you *know* it. I'm asking you if you *believe* it."

I felt like my last raw nerve had been exposed. Tears formed and puddled until all I saw of him was a blurred outline in the dim light of the study where we sat. I felt as if he had zapped me with some sort of gospel stun gun.

He waited for my reply patiently, and then he very quietly asked, "Well? Do you?" His tone was almost a whisper by this point.

I could only mutter a response. "This doesn't feel like love." The words barely made it past the lump in my throat, but I choked them out.

He smiled, nodded his head, and asked me why I thought I was not being loved. I unpacked my whole litany of pains I felt God was ignoring. I shared in very specific details what my wife's suffering looked like, what caring for her daily entailed, and how her disease had moved into our family and monopolized our lives. I shared how I drank at God, at her disease, and at my ineptitude to deal with it all. I unpacked the struggles with leadership I had in my church situation and the revolving door of staff members. I owned up to drinking at them as well. I bluntly told him that it seemed to me we all try to sell a God of healing and restoration, but it isn't true. God doesn't touch people and heal them. Not physically like in my wife's world, not psychologically like my drinking world, and not emotionally when it all hits the fan, especially when it comes to a teenaged daughter who has written me off. I wanted to be delivered *from*—not *through*—my circumstances.

This was not love! I would never do this to *my* daughter and call it "love!"

"Do you ever see Jesus as grieving with you in this?" Father Bennett asked. The tone of his voice remained hushed.

"Which Jesus?" I replied.

"Interesting," he said. "What do you mean by that?"

"I don't know which Jesus to buy into anymore," I replied. "I think I'm torn between the Jesus who was perfect, the Jesus who is pissed off at everyone else for not being, and the Jesus who lurks in the background talking in riddles. I totally believe it took incomprehensible love to hang on the cross for me, but do I see him grieving with me in this? No ... No ... I don't know ... Probably not."

"Then you don't know the Jesus of the Bible," he said with a bit more emphasis. "Read the Gospels. Look at Jesus the person, not the one-dimensional comic book hero he's painted into most of the time. This is a fully human man who knew joy, loss, grief, pain, excitement, and laughter. He loved to party, and could still sit with someone and, in an instant, have them unwrapping their stories to him.

"The real person of Jesus grieves with you about all of this, including your broken ways of trying to cope with it. He never *wanted* this for you, David. When he took on sin upon his death, he took on everything that got you where you are right now. He is very acquainted with this, as well as how you feel about it.

"Talk about feeling abandoned? He gets it. He gets *you*. Perfectly. What he longs for is to experience the joy *of* you.

"I know that things are still a bit fresh for you to be able to embrace all this in one moment but there will be a day when you see this Jesus and when you do it will change the way you view everything else."

I left that conversation restless and discontent, wrestling with how those implications had played out already in my life on so many levels. If my secret notions about all these things had been hiding out in my psyche, completely unchallenged and embalmed in several years' worth of rum and Diet Coke, was it any wonder I was more spiritually bankrupt than I ever thought?

Suffice it to say, I spent the next couple of days unpacking all our previous conversations and then trying to piece them back together. As I reflect on those days, I believe God put the monk in this fork in the road of my life to help me add the shards of faith back into my story and to challenge me in the concept of the God I thought I served, the Jesus I thought I knew, and the grace I thought I'd experienced.

There was much more to my visit over those few days, and we addressed many other issues. But when I left, I did so with permission to view things with a little less certainty and a little more mystery. I left with some new questions to chew on instead of merely kicking around my old answers. I've always been more of a mystic anyway. I'm very comfortable with that. I've faked certainty to avoid conflict most of my life, but I'm pretty much a mystery gazer disguised as a cynic.

As the days wound down and my time with the monks drew to a close, I had a short parting conversation with Father Bennett. Before leaving, I told him that all my life I had wanted to please God and find peace. That's really all the drinking was for me—just an attempt to find peace. I really thought I could. I told him I even used to joke that I never understood people praying for peace when Bacardi sold it for $9.99 a bottle.

Father Bennett chuckled and paused. He then offered this insight: "Well, now you have come to a fork in the road about what real peace is, who your 'true self' is, and at the same time you are beginning to embrace the fact that you're already perfectly acceptable to God. You came to that fork when you decided to get sober. Now what you have to do is embark on the things that will reveal peace to you and trust the process as you begin the miracle of living soberly. Soberly, meaning that you don't try to control life, that you understand what is and isn't your responsibility, and that you daily ask for the gift of his wisdom and build in enough silence to hear him speak.

"It takes time. Don't let anyone tell you otherwise. And it is not cheap, this peace we seek."

With that, he gave me a parting hug as he did at the end of each of our sessions during those days, and he spoke a blessing over me. I found the hug and the blessing as comforting as his guidance and insights. I think we Protestants should adopt that practice of speaking blessings over one another. It is like a balm for the soul when we speak a blessing over a life. It is both humbling and empowering to the one who receives it.

I returned to the monastery once a month for a day retreat with Father Bennett over the next six months until Tricia experienced the first of her series of serious falls and broken bones. The complications of my life as a caregiver were about to escalate to proportions I never could have anticipated.

Nonetheless, I firmly believe that I never would have looked at them from the same perspective had I not encountered my monk friend at the fork in the road.

chapter six
The Angst
of Relief

*The desert shatters the soul's arrogance and
leaves body and soul crying out in thirst and hunger.
In the desert we trust God or die.*

DAN B. ALLENDER, *THE HEALING PATH*

I see a counselor, Margaret, regularly. Her clients are largely made up of people who struggle with alcohol, chemical abuse and addiction. Her practice has focused on the world of treatment centers for the recovery community in the greater Nashville area and she has helped me through most of my eleven-plus years of sobriety. Her credentials are both medical and psychiatric. She also possesses a major dose of what my dad calls good, common horse sense.

At one point, she had an office on Music Row in Nashville, which I told her was like asking for walk-in traffic! I jokingly accused her of trying to be the Great Clips of addiction therapy. Margaret has challenged me, irritated me, and comforted me in just about every session over these many years.

A few months before my wife passed away, Margaret sat down with me and, as she is prone to do, she acted very harmless at first by putting on her counselor face and listening intently. As I babbled on about how difficult it was to place Tricia in hospice care, play the dating game with grief, and generally commiserated about how much of my own life I had lost in the span of time Tricia had been ill, Margaret became noticeably quiet. After a long pause, she said, "I want to ask you a question and I want you to really think about it before you answer. Are you prepared for the anxiety and void you are going to experience when Tricia finally passes?"

Without missing a beat, I said, "Margaret, you are great at what you do—and I even still like you. I will tell you that I am prepared to feel many things when that happens. I know I am going to experience grief and loss, and I even expect to experience a lot of loose ends. I may even experience relief and I am giving myself permission to feel that. But what I am *not* going to be is *anxious*. This has just been way too hard. Tricia has been in that hospital bed at home for seven years and I've taken care of her every single day. We've had this disease taking up space in our lives for eighteen years and it has been the centerpiece of our family. I drank at it, cussed at it, have thrown things at it. God and I have had it out in more ways than I can even recount. But what I am not going to feel is *anxious*."

Margaret smiled politely, gave me the counselor nod and said, "Okay, okay, we can talk about it later. It's just that sometimes our adversity can begin to define us. When we lose that role or something suddenly shifts, it can produce a lot of anxiety because we aren't sure who we are anymore. There is a lot of energy behind grief and caregiving and it will need somewhere to go. Just keep it in mind."

It is in some of those confounding moments that I add up all the money I've paid her and wonder if she has a return policy.

About six months after that conversation, on a Monday evening, Tricia passed away. I had already decided to donate her bed, power wheelchair and Hoyer lift to our hospice service. On Tuesday morning I called them to arrange pickup. They offered to come later in the week insisting that there was no rush.

In reply, I said, "No, I'd really like for you to come today actually." They agreed and I checked calling them off my list.

On Wednesday morning at around 4:30 I woke up and felt the need to clean out the walk-in closet that had all her medical supplies in it. I pulled things from shelves and dumped out drawers into big black trash bags I'd brought in. The items we could donate I placed in one bag and the stuff we couldn't I took to the garbage. *Poof!* Thank God I wasn't experiencing any of that pesky anxiety Margaret had warned me about.

By Thursday, the day of Tricia's memorial service, I had a big empty bedroom, an empty walk-in closet and absolutely nothing to do. There I was with no one watching the clock or waiting for me to get home. There were no meds to keep track of or care rituals of any kind to perform. In fact, there were no expectations on me for anything whatsoever. I had prayed that God would either heal Tricia here or heal her in heaven and he chose to heal her in heaven. I consider that a miracle, but it was after the miracle that things became interesting.

Ever since I was a young boy growing up in the church I have loved the miracle stories. I have cheered as we got to the "take up your bed and walk" endings and imagined the awestruck crowds murmuring in disbelief. In the movies, the violins swell and the angels sing ... which makes for an epic moment, especially for the guy on the bed. But here is where I think beyond the scriptures a bit. Whether we are talking about the man being lowered through the roof, or the man hanging out at the pool of Bethesda for thirty-eight years waiting on someone to help him into the healing waters, both men encountered the same situation after the miracle. They were both faced with who they would be and what life would look like from that point on. They both potentially faced the anxiety of relief.

First, I must say this about the man at the pool—*really*? Thirty-eight *years* and you couldn't get someone to help drag your sorry behind into the water?

Then we have the man on the mat, the other guy who is so desperate that his friends are cutting holes in the roof. I picture the homeowner on the ground yelling up, "I'm pretty sure this isn't covered by my homeowners" as they lower their friend in to see Jesus. This is a man so desperate, he is borrowing the faith of his friends just to get there.

As those of us familiar with the passage know, Jesus says, "Take up your bed and walk." But *first* he says, "Your sins are forgiven" which is really the *big* miracle and ironically the one we often pass over. Why are we more excited about being well than being forgiven?

Maybe it has something to do with the fact that we are clueless as to just how broken we are.

I have this idea that the man rolled up his bed and headed for home. As he ambled along on his newly remodeled legs, he began to realize some things about his new reality. *"I am going to need a job. I don't have a way to make a living. My mom has been taking care of me since I was a kid* (or got hit by the ox cart, or whatever happened to him). *My mom's whole identity is caring for me. She's going to have a complete identity crisis and that's not going to be fun. Who am I going to be from here? All my excuses are eliminated! People are going to expect more from me than they ever have and I don't know how to do being well. I know how to do being sick."*

Those Bible stories play out in my mind whenever I relive the conversation with Margaret as she reminded me, "David, in your relationship as a caregiver, you've been able to hide behind this disease of Tricia's. Everything you haven't wanted to confront and everything you haven't wanted to change in your life, every chance you haven't wanted to take that you say is important to you but haven't done—you have had the perfect reason to avoid those things and nobody is going to blame you, nor should they. But that's gone. If you don't like your job anymore, if you don't like where you live, or you want to be whatever when you grow up, guess what. You're going to get the opportunity to confront it now. Not to mention the issue of relationships."

This is scary stuff! So, when I hear Jesus say, "Do you want to be well?" I don't hear him say, "Do you want to walk?" I hear him say, "Do you want to embrace a new way of living and being and thinking and surrendering that is going to come with an even bigger miracle? The miracle of freedom. The miracle of finally knowing your *true self*."

That is a whole different question.

Frankly, I believe that there are some days when we would rather be back on the mat where, regardless of its hardships, at least life was predictable. When I was on the mat I knew who I was, what was expected of me, and there wasn't this new blank, white canvas which is now my life giving me snow blindness while I stare it down.

For some of us, the mat looks like different things. It's not necessarily a physical malady. Some of us have been on the mat of resentment, the mat of anger, the mat of being unforgiving, or the mat of blaming our fractured marriages. We fear if we give up that mat we won't know who we are anymore because we've been on it for so long. The mat has become our identity just as much as the paralyzed man, the addict, or the caregiver. If we surrender that, we don't know who we will be ... and that is a fearfully desperate place to be.

Many of us approach that fear by garnering the prayerful support of our friends and family, which can be a good thing. Unfortunately, what I often see happen in prayer groups is that we only pray for the miracle. We get all our prayer requests together—so and so who is going through a divorce, so and so has cancer, so and so have kids who are rebellious, and on it goes.

We pray, "God, heal this marriage. God, just make these kids compliant—give them hearts for you. Lord, do a miracle in our finances." What we don't consider is that a prayer for a miracle is actually a prayer for desperation. The healed lepers, the guy on the roof, and even the guy at the pool are all people who knew the *gift* of desperation. Instead, we sit in our groups and pray for this benign "touch it, heal it, fix it" God to zap us sober or wave his hand and take away our pain ... and frankly, he may or may not.

The harder prayer to pray addresses how we got on the mat in the first place. Or, where we would go if we were to take up our beds and walk. That prayer would sound more like, "God, reveal to me the resentments I carry that are fueling my entitlement that is allowing me to justify my behavior. Behavior, which is hurting myself and others around me."

Most days I don't like to pray that prayer very much. I want the "zap me" prayer. "God, just give me compliant children and a happy spouse!" That's the prayer I want to pray. I don't want to pray about my resentments and my entitlement and my whole ability to deceive myself in my own life. I just want to walk! I want my friends to walk. I want my marriage to walk.

But what God shows us about himself in these situations is that he does some beautiful work through gifts of desperation and, eventually, gratitude that actually make us *well*.

The scriptures in Luke say that when the lepers come to Jesus and are being healed only one comes back to thank him. And when he comes back to Jesus, he falls on his face and worships out of the gratitude I referred to earlier. His desperation and need brought him to Jesus. His realization of his new state of being brought him to gratitude, and his gratitude brought him to worship.

There are two things I believe are missing in the church today: desperation and gratitude. We are not *that* desperate to be in worship and we are honestly not *that* grateful. If we were, our worship would look different, and I don't mean that more of us would be raising our hands. I really believe we are not embracing the desperation and gratitude that goes with "your sins are forgiven, take up your bed and walk."

Desperation and gratitude intersecting is what worship is.

So, when we ask God to reveal those resentments, for example, we demonstrate surrender, and it is in our surrender that we acknowledge desperation and experience gratitude, and therefore encounter true worship.

A rather famous photograph emerged after the bombing of Sarajevo in 1992—the image of a man named Vedran Smailovic.

He is now known as the cellist of Sarajevo. Twenty-two people in Vedran's community lost their lives in one incident, most of them standing outside a bakery waiting for it to open. "My mother is a Muslim and my father is a Muslim," Mr. Smailovic said, "but I don't care. I am a Sarajevan, I am a cosmopolitan, I am a pacifist." Then he added: "I am nothing special, I am a musician, I am part of the town. Like everyone else, I do what I can."[2]

With that in mind, he put on his concert black tails, packed up his cello and played beautiful pieces of music, such as "Adagio in G Minor" from the heaps of rubble. Not for one day, but for twenty-two days—one day for every life lost in his community. He said that in the midst of this destruction and this desperation, in the midst of this hopelessness, the only gift he could offer was hope in the form of beauty. So, from the heaps of rock and rubble, desperation and gratitude intersected. The sound was of music and the miracle of healing beginning.

Jesus tells us to take up our bed and walk, but first he asks us if we want to be well. Are we willing to surrender our beds to the music of healing? Can we surrender our anger, our resentment? Can we surrender that thing we are holding on to which has been defining us? The thing that stands between us, and all that we say we believe?

Jesus is chasing all of us. What we didn't expect was that he is chasing us in an '87 Bronco with bad suspension.

I wanted Jesus to show up on the white horse, but he didn't. I wanted to be whisked up and taken off to a straight, smooth road into the sunset. I wanted him to zap me sober and zap my wife well. Just change our circumstances and life will look okay again. Right? If he would have just given me my old life back, I could have done this on my own.

What is this big thing Jesus has about "being needed" anyway?

So, Jesus drives up in his '87 Bronco (wearing a flannel shirt by the way), and asks us to get in the passenger side. And Jesus is a terrible driver! He doesn't stay on his side of the road. He doesn't have a GPS and he's one of those people who faces you to talk while he drives and he never really looks at the road because he knows where he is going and he likes to say "trust me" a lot. This is how he rolls while we hang on for dear life. In those moments, we find ourselves saying, "*This* is the Christian life? What about the big white horse and the open road and the angels and the violins and the 'take up your bed and walk' guy?"

But Jesus says (calmly, I should add), "Trust me, trust me. Surrender."

And all the while, I am learning that a bumpy road in a Bronco with Jesus is better than a wide-open road with me driving in a Lamborghini because I have no idea where I'm going or how to get there.

Are we aware that desperation *is* the miracle? Do we realize that when we sit with one another in our desperation, we are experiencing a miracle in progress? Do we remind one another that this desperation will lead us to gratitude and that gratitude brings us to the true miracle of worship? The visible miracle, the "take up your bed and walk" miracle—that's not really the main point of the stories. **The true miracle is *after the miracle* when desperation and gratitude intersect.**

Are we willing to be well, to let God redefine us, reshape us, and renew us? Can we trust him enough to let go of our mats and walk into the miracle of the life that awaits us?

2   *The New York Times:* The Death of a City: Elegy for Sarajevo -- A special report.; A People Under Artillery Fire Manage to Retain Humanity, by John F. Burns, Published June 8, 1992.

chapter seven
From Here...
—Part 1—

A miracle is when the whole is greater than the sum of its parts. A miracle is when one plus one equals a thousand.

FREDERICK BUECHNER,
THE ALPHABET OF GRACE

I am convinced that the most *spiritual* things I do often seem to be the least "spiritual." It isn't in my passionate, euphoric crescendos of worship, the amount of stimulating inspirational literature I consume, or the level of emotional zeal during the many fervent prayer meetings in which I have participated that most effectively shape who I am becoming. Instead, experience tells me that when I engage in the most mundane, ordinary, and often gritty happenings around me, I begin to embrace what it means to live a surrendered life and ultimately experience God in his distressing disguise (as Mother Teresa said). Experiencing God wrapped in the rags of circumstances I would never have chosen—or want to do again—seem to be the times I have fallen most deeply into his embrace ... albeit often kicking and screaming. In the most profound agony of loss, doubt, and even loneliness is where I have experienced myself to be the most held and comforted and therefore the most honest and intimate with my Creator.

Even in the terminal isolation of my grief, the times when I bang myself against the rocks of my brokenness, I am reminded yet again that my most sacred space is right where I am, at this moment, as I take up the cross of my reality. Taking up my cross during Tricia's final days consisted of me feeding her a few bites of mashed sweet potatoes with a spoon, offering sips of water from a straw, and reminding her of where she was and who the people closest to her were. I rehearsed my own paraphrased scripture passages to myself as if to hear Jesus saying to me, "Take up your spoon and follow me. Take up your wife's bursting urine bag and be my disciple. They will know you are my follower by your changing of soiled bed linens." When I boil it all down I believe that those daily, unenviable details are exactly what Jesus means by taking up a cross. This is when we realize that it is Love that has shackled us to these circumstances and Love that gives us our next breath while we walk in them.

The isolation of our grief—the lie that our pain is so foreign and unique that we want to hide like Cro-Magnon cave dwellers to survive—is coupled with the fear of continuing life without this individual sharing it with us. This reality is contrasted by a tear-stained joy knowing that their tattered tent of a body will soon be discarded and they will one day be perfectly whole and miraculously free. Hence the exhausting and bewildering dance we do with grief. This is in its purest state a miracle, but never the one we pray for.

Being a witness to the encroaching and inevitable loss of a loved one from a neurological disease is like watching the person you love get eaten by gnats. It isn't swift and merciful. Instead, it devours a person piece by tiny piece, function by simple function, and glimmer by twinkling glimmer until what is left is the shell of someone you've never met.

Tricia's strong soprano voice that had once belted out beautiful operatic musical pieces when she was a voice major at Baylor University was now reduced to a faint, warbling whisper accompanied by the slurred speech and exaggerated enunciation of a person who found her words hard to call forth. The keen mind that once helped organize business exchange programs between the United States and Japan for the engineering department at Vanderbilt University could no longer discern the simplest children's games on her laptop computer. What used to be a completely independent and confident woman now called out to me fearfully in the middle of the night to inform me that her phone wasn't working as she handed me what turned out to be the TV remote control.

I felt as if I had been a *caregiver* for the full extent of our married life, which in fact wasn't true. But the constant and daily nature of caregiving can find one believing that this is all one has ever known. Whenever I was identified as a caregiver, the roles in my brain shifted from *husband* (the guy who loved bringing her flowers on her birthday and surprising her with dessert from her favorite bakery) to the person showing up for work in some brightly clad version of scrubs and squeaky white shoes. In my role as a caregiving spouse it was easy for me to think that I had already spent my most sorrowful days pouring over the inventory of our losses. I had adopted the notion that I could pay ahead on my grief like we do a mortgage or our credit card balances. I had convinced myself that by the time we would reach the final stretch of Tricia's anguished life, I would have grieved the bulk of my loss and have it neatly folded and stored away.

I reasoned that I had begun losing her a long time ago. After all, I hadn't had a *wife* in any kind of traditional sense for many years. Somewhere along the way, I began to see Tricia more as my sick aunt than my spouse. Maybe it was a way of emotionally detaching. One never wants anything to happen to a sick aunt and we will lovingly care for her to the end, but the essence of a *wife* left me long before I had to lay her to rest physically. The image of who we had been together, what the *us* part of marriage meant, and the dreams we had yet to see to fruition were realities I thought I had tidily packed away in their respective cubicles as closed cases. I was blindsided by the anxiety, loss of identity, and sheer regret that awaited me on the other side of her passing, in light of my overestimating the validity of pay-ahead grief.

In Tricia's last weeks with us she was no longer able to feed herself. Her hands and arms were virtually useless as her MS progressed upward. Her cognitive state became very compromised and she would often find herself in a frustrated state of perplexity about this or that. She experienced episodes that found her holding on to imaginary objects and reaching up as if to be handing them to me. I would smile and take them from her hand and thank her for giving them to me. She would smile back as if she had full confidence in my understanding what to do with the nonexistent articles.

This is what dying looks like. It sucks with a loud noise! It isn't graceful. It isn't sweet. And it sure as hell isn't pretty. Speaking from the perspective of my human heart, I would have to say that death's waiting room is a *really* crappy place to have to spend any time.

It was in those long, silent hours where I had nothing left to give that I learned that Love could do what I cannot. In the sacredness of the mundane, the loneliness, and my most *daily* moments, I realized that the biggest piece to loving someone is simply being present.

As I watched her struggle to eat from the spoon God entrusted to me, my heart would quietly hope that the tiny bites of food she received from me reminded her at some level that I loved her, that I was still there for her and that she mattered. Even as my heart's core begged to be anywhere else, I knew that I was exactly where God meant for me to be in that moment, and it was hallowed, right, and precious. It is in the things as seemingly mundane as five bites of mashed sweet potatoes that God shows himself.

Tricia's final days were marked by throngs of friends, family, and church people who wanted to spend a few rare moments with her recapturing memories and reliving more pleasant times. Her bedroom was a place of perpetual songs, flowers, laughter, tears, and prayers. Our home became a revolving door of smiles, sadness, hospice teams, and hugs. My freezer was so stocked by generous, southern families that we ended up having to turn down meals.

The reality of dying in the south is that we provide the grieving family enough food to eat their way through all the so-called stages of grief ten times over. We like to give things that freeze well because apparently one never knows when such severe pangs of bereavement will strike that only a hash brown casserole can console. Families have been known to obliterate entire chocolate cakes and pans of banana pudding at the very sight of a hearse. Despite our quirky, southern customs, there is not a more loving place in all the earth to pass away from this life. You will be sung to, read to, held, caressed, and embraced until your last breath leaves you.

Early on Monday morning, May 6, 2013, I walked into Tricia's bedroom to get her turned and sitting upright for the day. We had been through a very long weekend where she was not able to stay alert. She had begun drifting in and out of deep sleeplike states for longer and longer periods. She wasn't eating, wasn't taking in much liquid, and things seemed to be shutting down rather quickly. As I approached her bedside I noticed that her blanket was soiled and that she had regurgitated in her sleep. She was breathing normally and not in any distress, but I immediately called our hospice nurse who told me that he would arrive first thing.

As I proceeded to clean her up, change her gown, and remove her sheets I noticed that her body was extremely cold. Her lips, fingertips and toes had begun to turn blue and she had a very pale hue to her skin. She responded to me but only in a semi-conscious state. I decided the best thing to do was to continue cleaning her up if only to make sure she was comfortable until our nurse arrived.

By the time the hospice nurse and his nurse-tech arrived, Tricia had slipped into a deep sleeplike state once again. Tom, our nurse, examined her. Her body temperature had dropped significantly. Her blood pressure was also extremely low and her heart rate had slowed as well.

After examining her more closely and commenting on the bluish tint to her fingers, toes, and lips he looked up at me and motioned me to come with him. As we stood outside the bedroom doorway Tom lovingly, but sternly whispered, "I think you should call anyone you think would like to see Tricia and tell them that they should come *today*. I don't mean tomorrow *if* they can drop by. I mean *today*. She's going home soon."

After eighteen years of her disease it still confounds me how unprepared I was to hear those words. I knew I would hear them one day, and after the nature of her last few days I knew it would be soon. Regardless, I still felt my heart drop when I heard Tom *say* those words to me. Out loud.

I remember thinking, "Wait! We're not ready. Are you sure?"

Tom perceived my startled expression, and in his usual calm and reassuring manner said, "We knew this was coming, didn't we? Would you mind if we had a word of prayer around Tricia before we start administering the morphine?" I nodded and went to get our daughter, Lauren, from another part of the house. She was chatting with my sister, Jackie, who had dropped in earlier. Jackie, Lauren, our nurse tech, and Tom all reached around me as we encircled Tricia's bed. Tom led in a pastoral prayer of comfort. His prayer painted a picture of God holding Tricia and restoring her and renewing her perfectly.

This was not a prayer where we all locked arms and agreed to tell God what he was obligated to do. It was a prayer of grief acknowledging that God's ways were not ours, that his timing is perfect, that we are hurting, and that we are committing this process to him in any way that he chooses to move in it.

From that moment on it was as if I lived that day from ten thousand feet above the ground. I literally felt as though I watched it *all* happen and it wasn't even 8:00 a.m. I immediately called one of our dearest friends, Cindy, who was the Director of Congregational Care at our church. She and her team are the Navy Seals of personal crisis. Once she arrived I didn't have to make a single decision or phone call. She alerted our church leadership and as the word began to trickle, people randomly showed up at our home. Over the course of the day we had at least sixty people drop in. Tricia was never *really* conscious after that morning, but the visitors all prayed over her, brushed her hair, kept her lips moist with swabs, and even sang to her. We had a CD playing in her room that I'd made for her—a compilation of some of her favorite music, some of my piano music, and various songs she had sung over the years.

As the day dragged on I could feel the energy draining away from my body. The entire day had felt like a family dinner that wouldn't end. My best friend, Jonathan, had been with me all day. His family joined us late that afternoon for dinner and his wife Jenny took over organizing some of the food storage and meal plans we were offered. Everyone pitched in and made things happen around me as I watched my life play out from some emotionally distant perch.

Our nurse practitioner friend, Julie, helped me seek out hospice care months earlier, organized Tricia's Wednesday "lunch ladies," and made sure Tricia always had plenty of visits and contact with people over the last months of her isolating illness. Julie was always on hand with good medical input and she willingly spent the night with Tricia when I had to be out of town. She was another person without whom I couldn't have made it through the last few years, let alone the months and weeks prior to losing Tricia. She was a part of that day as well, helping us process what was physically happening and how to anticipate the next several hours.

As evening came, the traffic through our home began to subside and the foreboding feeling of the night settled in around us. Julie offered to stay up with Tricia and let Lauren and me get some sleep. Jonathan and his family had gone home by then because, at that point, it looked as if Tricia might last through the night. Our immediate families had gone back home as well.

Lauren and I were winding down in the living room going through family albums and scrapbooks. We found solace picking out pictures and memorable photos that we knew would make a great montage of memories honoring the essence of Tricia's life.

By around 10:15, Julie called from the bedroom to Lauren and me. When we got to the room we saw that Tricia had begun a deep, heaving kind of breathing that was staggered with long pauses between breaths. Julie said that this type of breathing happens immediately before people pass and that we should stay with her and she would give us this time alone. As Julie made her way out of the bedroom Lauren and I curled up on each side of Tricia in her hospital bed and held her.

The CD that had been looping all day still played quietly in the corner. The song playing was a piano piece I had written for Tricia many years before, and recorded on my first instrumental project, "More Than Words: A Theme for Tricia." Candles burned and only a dim lamp in the corner illuminated the room. Lauren and I held Tricia's hands and began to simply converse with her. We told her we loved her and we were going to be okay. I reminded Tricia that I was the man I was because she had believed in me more than I had most of the time. This was not the first time I had shared those words with her, but it seemed fitting to express them again. She heaved and sighed another laborious breath. Lauren and I waited to see if she would inhale again.

She eventually did.

I leaned in and whispered, "We're going to be okay, Sweet Pea. And you're going to be okay, too. This is all going to be okay. It's okay to let go." I kissed her cold forehead as she exhaled.

She never drew breath back into her body after that. She left us for heaven at 10:30 that warm Monday night in May beneath a beautiful quilt made especially for her by a lady in our church named Barbara.

I waited for her to draw another breath for what felt like an eternity, but my spirit knew she was gone. My heart and my soul were bearing witness to it. The vacuum of her absence was as real as if she had gotten up and physically left the room. Moments passed and I leaned in and lay across her cold body and began to embrace her. I wept like I had never wept in my life. I didn't even recognize the sounds pouring from me. What gushed out of me was a visceral spew of prayers, sobs, and chant-like repetitions.

"It's over. It's over. It's over..."

My tears soaked Tricia's cool neck and chest. I remember screaming to Jesus that he had to take her and love her for me and that this hope of heaven had all better be real because we had put everything we have and are into believing this. I reminded him that Tricia had lived too many miserable years for this to turn out not to be true in the end.

These are the ultimate forks in the road of life when we will either collapse in faith, or we will collapse into despair. But, either way we collapse. Faith will embrace us in our tears and we find Comfort there. Despair is literally hell because it has nothing to offer and we are alone in it.

As I looked up from embracing Tricia's lifeless body, I reached out to Lauren. We stood over her mother embracing and weeping together. What we experienced in that moment together took days of processing before we could really articulate it, even to one another. Joy, sorrow, pain, freedom, relief for her, relief for us, the deepest loss of our lives, ... the emotions were endless. I have never been the same since that night and I realize now that I never will. It is more than a defining moment or a watermark by which we will remember a date. It is the instant my life changed courses, the instant my story was irreversibly altered.

I now entered the *after Tricia died* phase of my life.

chapter eight
From Here...
—Part 2—

History, despite its wrenching pain, cannot be unlived,
however, if faced with courage, need not be lived again.
MAYA ANGELOU

*I*n the days, weeks and months *after Tricia died,* processing my thoughts was like being inside of one of those wind machines where people win money by snatching at the swirling dollar bills blowing around inside. My thoughts spun around me; only some of them did I manage to retain.

I'm not one who considers myself to be scattered by nature. I have never been diagnosed with ADD or had to take meds to help me focus. Yet, in those first few weeks, simple tasks like starting the washing machine but forgetting to put in the clothes, walking away leaving the oven door hanging open, or never putting away the entire bottom rack of dishes from the dishwasher were common occurrences. I showed up for appointments on the wrong days more than a few times because I couldn't seem to enter dates in my calendar accurately.

Some details I carried out fine. Others were left to blow around in my foggy brain as I clutched at them only to find they had slipped through my grasp.

The botched logistics have been the easy things to contend with. After so many years of being oriented to watching the clock to make sure I was home in time to turn Tricia in her bed or make sure she had her lunch or took her medicine, I felt out of sorts when I realized those tasks were no longer necessary. Nothing took me as long as it used to.

At first, I woke up every morning thinking I should go check on her first thing. I frequently reached for my phone to call her to see if I could bring her anything from the store. When I sat down in the living room I would have to remind myself that she wouldn't be lonesome in the back of the house without me coming in to spend the evening with her. I no longer had to offer to share my dessert, make sure to charge her laptop, or turn in my orders for her medical supplies. Every time I encountered (and continue to encounter) the opportunity to remember each of those things, I am reminded that I am different.

While going through closets, drawers, the attic, and her keepsakes, I find myself wanting to ask her if she thinks we should save something. When is it okay to throw away a person's hairbrush? What do you do with keepsakes that meant more to the person you lost than they ever did to you?

Is it okay to finally admit that I never liked the color of our hall bathroom even though she did? Can I finally get rid of all the books she saved because she thought that she might want to read them again? What do I do about her nightstand drawer that smells like her hand lotion and the fact that I can't bear to open it?

The feelings of being displaced are perplexing in that I'm not the one who actually *went* anywhere and yet I feel as if my whole life is foreign to me. I am a bit like the man who went to sleep on an airplane and missed his connection. When he got off the plane he expected to be in Cleveland and instead found himself in San Diego. He loves the weather in San Diego but he lives in Cleveland. He can predict the weather in Cleveland. He has no idea what people do in San Diego.

As nice as it is there, he didn't ask to end up in San Diego.

And neither did I.

However, the real glitch in the analogy is that in real life there are still flights back to Cleveland if you end up in San Diego. My reality is that I will never experience life in Cleveland again. From now on, I am going to have to learn what it is like to live as a foreign man in a foreign place.

From here I will learn to adapt to my new surroundings. From here I will eventually adapt to the new time zone where a week feels like a month. And from here, I'm praying for someone in San Diego to befriend me and teach me my way around. From here I must eventually learn to accept that life moved on for everyone but me.

A dear friend of mine, a young woman who lost her husband unexpectedly, told me that the first weeks would actually be the easy part. She warned me about the day when things simmered down and I would be alone in my grief. It didn't happen right away, but she was right. There is ultimately a time when everyone goes back to their lives, their jobs, their families, and you don't. I soon realized how right she was as it became clear to me that the person I had been was no longer required. Rather than experiencing relief in that little epiphany, I found it left me anxious and isolated.

Surely somebody in San Diego needed to be taken care of!

From here, grief shows up dressed up like other things. Loss disguised as angst. Sadness introduced herself in the form of anger hoping I didn't recognize her with all the makeup. Loneliness masqueraded as busyness thinking I might not identify him easily if he didn't stand still long enough. I soon realized my fulltime job was to take every emotion I thought I was experiencing and look behind it.

The feelings on the surface are always the easy ones. I know how to push through fear. I can manage anger and rage. Kicking anxiety in the butt is just a matter of some good self-talk, right?

But, the emotions behind the emotions, the ones grief likes to impersonate, are much harder to pinpoint. Deep sadness, profound loss, relational pain, and loneliness simply must be sat in like a sauna until it wrings out every drop of our denial and misplaced energy to be able to properly identify them for what they are.

The days when I try not to be the guy who lost his wife are tough—and exhausting frankly. It takes a lot of energy to help put other people at ease in your presence. The days when grief lies to me and tells me that I'm forgotten and that no one wants to hear my story for the eleven-millionth time are paralyzing. The occasions when the deep wound is crying out to be medicated and my version of medicating is no longer an option are also rather baffling.

Ironically, I hadn't felt this raw since my first weeks of sobriety. How did God expect me to wake up, breathe in and out, put one foot in front of the other, and then do it all again, let alone start a *new normal* for myself?

How in the hell do these people in San Diego do it?

And why are people phrasing questions to me in ways that imply that my grief will be something I "get through"? Is there really a day when I am supposed to wake up and not miss Tricia or not grieve what we didn't get to have together? Is that what working *through* grief means?

I believe that rather than working *through* grief, we learn to work *with* it ... like learning to live *with* a missing limb. We learn to compensate for the missing limb and learn to use other methods to accommodate being without it. But every blessed day of the world we are keenly aware that we are missing *something*.

A friend of mine who lost her teenaged son in a car accident told me that for months when she would come home alone she would stand in the foyer and call out her son's name up the staircase because she liked how it sounded. She said that for one split second, hearing his name echoing off of the upstairs walls made life feel *normal* again. As she cried, she told me it was worth the pain she might experience afterward to get to relive a second of her former life hearing his name resonating through the house as if he would respond and come bounding down the stairs to greet her.

These are the heartbreaking stories that only grief can tell. Grief is not rational. It doesn't produce actions that *make sense*. Instead it causes us to grasp at anything that looks like it might offer one split second of relief from the chronic heartache that we carry, even if it is calling out names of our dead loved ones up empty staircases.

Four weeks after Tricia passed, Lauren bought a house. She had moved back home the previous year to save money for a down payment. Now, I can see the true blessing was beyond Lauren's financial blessing. This time gave her a year with her mother to heal wounds and enjoy being together. The evening I came home after moving Lauren into her new home I went back to her empty bedroom passing Tricia's empty room on the way. And then it hit me.

I was completely alone for the first time in my entire life. I lowered myself to sit on her bare hardwood floor, asking, "Where am I going to go from here?"

How do I just walk in to this cavernous place and turn on the television and pretend that my life isn't upside down? It is a bit like walking into a restaurant after an earthquake and asking them if they are still serving dinner. Here I am again trying to see Cleveland from San Diego.

From here, Cleveland feels like a world away.

One of the most touching expressions extended to me in my processing of life came from my friend and speaking agent Wes Yoder. Wes is also an author and long-time Nashville beacon of encouragement to many in the music, speaking, and entertainment worlds. On the one-year anniversary of Tricia's death he sent a poem he wrote for me which sums up beautifully the hope, confusion, and beauty of where I find myself today.

I Suppose

by Wes Yoder

for David, on the occasion of his sorrow and tears.

i suppose

in this place -

we who believe

will always feel the weight

of our schizophrenia,

being here while there,

being there while not there,

barely here,

holding close

those far away,

believing in doubt,

trusting what we cannot see

but feel,

and knew,

and somehow

know...

i suppose

when the ropes break

which keep us here,

when our love flies away to Jesus,

when sorrow says,

your turn,

where grief cannot complete

and happiness delays,

silence comes

with loving arms to hold us

i suppose...

i suppose

this insanity

is holy

and sacred...

I suppose,

then,

we shall be satisfied –

ok?

for now?

I suppose...

From here, I can see the days get a little longer and little brighter. The dreams of Tricia visiting me in the middle of the night just to talk and check in seem to have stopped for now. The seemingly disconnected thoughts and emotions have begun to settle in to their respective cubicles so I can visit them on my terms instead of on their haphazard terms. I am more at peace with my pain since I have begun to understand grief as an ongoing process instead of a crash course or a pay-ahead debt solution. My new normal is finally starting to *feel* normal. I still get lonely, but it doesn't show up disguised as a chocolate cake, at least not as often. My Great Pyrenees puppy I got two months after Tricia passed is now up to one hundred pounds. Her name is Lilly and she loves me and that's the full extent of her job description. Lauren is moving forward in her career and her personal life and yet still finds it necessary to come and have dinner with me once a week or so to check in and to give me advice. The joy of having adult children is that we can swap our grownup life stories now and share our grownup pain. Her caring heart for me is a testimony to God's redeeming work and a demonstration of grace beyond anything I deserve.

From here I will walk this road with the rock in my shoe— the tiny fragment that is left over from the most defining moments in my life as a reminder that God is faithful and that I am human. It reminds me of my need for His mercy daily, the meaning of surrender, and that peace, courage, and wisdom are mine for the asking. In a very uncomfortable way it reminds me that I am not alone, and that I am loved.

It is a token of my sacred insanity and the sanctity of coming to the end of myself.

chapter nine
Beyond the Mat

The glory of God is man fully alive.
ST. IRENAEUS

*S*ome of us are certainly more aware of our brokenness than others. And a few of us have that handful of honest friends who aren't afraid to point it out to us from time to time. These are the people I refer to as my "mat carriers," the ones who love me enough to cut a hole in the roof and lower me down to Jesus when I would rather stay unmoved on my ratty, stained, and tattered mat where life is safe and predictable.

These mat bearers are also my fellow travelers who help me make the journey after Jesus tells me to take up my mat and walk. This road *after the miracle* is not designed to be a solo trip. We need our mat carriers *after* the miracle even more than we did when we were sick or in crisis. We are about to become different people than those who inhabited the flea-infested pallets we called our reality before. We are about to experience a new way of being, thinking, and believing along with a whole new set of responsibilities and expectations in the real world—a place many of us have either avoided or been isolated from for as long as humanly possible.

Most of us are not aware when we embark on this journey of recovery, healing, and restoration that we come to it with a set of unspoken and unmet expectations. Bargains with God, promises to family and friends, and even our own set of impossible standards become fodder for resentments when we realize that the world isn't lining the streets to give us the parade we believe we deserve for our newly found freedom. It never occurred to us that becoming healthy and individualized from the identity of our sickness was going to bring unsteadiness to many of the relationships in our lives. And it most certainly didn't occur to those closest to us that our challenging the old relational patterns that kept us sick would result in upsetting the dance with the people we trained to help keep us that way.

I was surprised to realize that the first chapter of my coming alive would begin with the process of grieving my old ideas, grieving who I used to be, and grieving what had ultimately kept me sick. I found myself awakening to the reality that I had lived a performance-driven life. Not only vocationally and professionally, but even my entrenched, broken belief system and skewed Christian ideology left me feeling as if I had played the juggler for God's little garden parties. I constantly found myself coming home from church gatherings feeling out of breath, as if I had just sprinted the hundred-yard dash. I constantly felt that I had to be *on*, and if I wasn't, I had somehow let the world down. I eventually realized I was putting far more confidence in my persona—as if God needed a PR agent at the table—than I was interested in surrendering to what he wanted to do uniquely in me by his own Spirit.

I recall a Sunday (before I got sober) going to a restaurant with my wife and daughter after church. Tricia was still well enough to get out from time to time at that point and we had just come from two back-to-back Sunday morning services where I had led worship. After we had successfully asked half the establishment to rearrange their seating so that we could make the journey to a table on the dark side of the moon with Tricia's cumbersome wheelchair, our server introduced herself and asked if we would like anything from the bar.

I replied, "Yes, we'll have two glasses of your house Cabernet."

Tricia replied that she didn't care for any wine at lunch and I sharply informed her that they weren't for her. I shot a stern look back to our server and said, "They are for me. I just came from church."

As we truly become fully alive, we realize we have been living in a way that was never sustainable. Coming to grips with who we are going to be from here, especially without anesthesia, requires rethinking everything we thought we knew about God and our faith.

My first sponsor told me that Christians are "the hardest stinkin' people in the world to get sober" because we have been led to believe that we have God in a box. Add water, shake, and serve. We are used to spouting off Sunday school answers and quick fixes that don't hold up in our new paradigm where rigorous honesty is king.

Not to mention that the rest of the world doesn't know *what* we're talking about ... those of us who battle addiction, live with chronic illness, and suffer the tragic loss of loved ones don't have patience for the Hallmark version of the gospel anymore.

I soon realized I would only stay sober to the extent that I was willing to let go of the God I thought I knew and open myself up to the mystery and common grace of a God who was much bigger than I had allowed myself to imagine. In other words, it was time to hang up my tap shoes and sit down for some honest face-to-face time with the God of the universe and the true Jesus who will not only hand me Kleenex, but who will also weep with me.

My life on the mat of performance-driven faith had also made me a prisoner of my own secrets. Things I couldn't even admit to myself let alone God or anyone else. After life on the mat, I realized I had only been asking God to conform my behavior instead of change my heart. When it became clear that God wasn't going to support my moralistic approach to wellness by merely changing me on the outside, the only choice I saw was to become more private and secretive so I would fit into the system I had built a life around. Leaving behind the God I thought I knew and walking toward a God that could handle my truth was asking more than I thought I could really embrace at first.

As hard as it was to get sober, I found it harder to put my old ideas on the shelf and only gradually add back the pieces I could honestly own a little at a time. Sometimes I think it is easier to get an agnostic to embrace a God of his or her own understanding than to get an evangelical to let go of the God they think they already know.

My life on the mat required a version of God I could predict, one I could answer for and sell with the right branding. I had no idea at the time that worshipping a God who required me to perform was keeping me sick. I honestly believed that if God had just stayed in the box and behaved himself, everything would have been fine! Instead, he likes to get out and go for walks and stir the crap. That usually results in change, or at least some confrontation with the facts.

The facts were that I had tried to worship some twisted version of my own conjecture instead of the God who would rise to meet me where I lay. To embrace that kind of God would require the deepest, most fundamental trust of the heart.

Change always feels like loss. There is a very real span of grieving that comes over us as our old ideas begin to give way to new ways of being, especially when it involves parting ways with a substance. This is often misinterpreted as a crisis of faith or even losing our faith. It feels like depression, looks like indifference, and sounds like cynicism. It is none of those. It is simply losing the illusion of certainty. When we drop our personas and become honest with ourselves, it upsets the playing field for everyone around us because it calls *their* personas into question as well. Many avoid this scenario in the name of peacemaking instead of embracing the fact that sometimes people just need to feel uncomfortable.

I am told by friends who work with me in the field of addiction therapy that once a partner gets into recovery the divorce rate is *higher* than when the addicts are active in their chronic addiction. Before the *miracle*, the relationship "worked," even in its most miserable state, because both parties were willing to play their respective roles. For instance, no one wants to be an alcoholic or an addict and certainly no one wants to be married to one. Both parties are trying equally hard for this reality to not be true and will support one another in that illusion in their respective ways as long as it is humanly possible. Once it becomes completely undeniable that there is a problem and the sick partner asks for help, it is as if the tide turns and the plates of the earth shift positioning everyone involved for the perfect storm.

The newly sober person eventually develops opinions, ideas, boundaries, and a stronger sense of self than they've most likely ever displayed throughout their entire relationship. The spouse or partner who constantly carried the ball and covered for the sick and/or addicted partner is faced with a new role to play. Now, the old version of who they had been is no longer as necessary or even wanted. The addict has found his or her voice and the spouses and partners feel as though they are gradually losing theirs. The addict wants to be celebrated for the progress they make along the road to freedom and the partner feels they can barely catch up. The trust level during this new pink cloud of sobriety is very low on the part of the person who has watched their loved one swing away at this dragon of addiction a thousand times and lose. The addict wants a parade lauding their newly found freedom and the family may feel only cautiously optimistic at best.

My good friend and fellow author, Nate Larkin, describes life for the partner of an addict as being like someone who gets hit by a bus and all the passersby flock to the driver to see if he's okay. The spouse is lying in the street bleeding and bruised while the addict/driver is the focus of all the energy on the scene.

I have seen and even experienced the same principles with caregiving and chronic illness. We often see caregivers lose themselves and completely immerse themselves in the lives of a loved one suffering with a serious and even terminal illness. It is a constant merry-go-round of logistical organizing, learning new medical procedures to be performed at home, dispensing medicine at the prescribed hours, and arranging care for every minute that one needs to be away from the home. Every meal, every clean sheet, and every obligation their children may have lands on them as they become completely given over to the needs of everyone but themselves. Oddly, when the cancer goes into remission or their loved one takes a sudden turn for the better, there is often a tension that presents itself as the caregiver's identity and role is challenged. The partner who experienced the disease wants to exert their new independence and make life work on his or her own terms again.

The caregiving spouse has had a complete shift in what is expected of them and awakens one day only to realize that they have lost themselves to the point that they don't even know their own favorite color, if they have a hobby, or even recall the last time they went to a movie. Meanwhile, the church, their friends, and the world around them are praising God for the miracle of a cancer free diagnosis for their spouse and telling them how relieved they must be to not have all the grueling responsibilities that had been a part of their reality all those months and even years prior.

When the miracle alters our identities, whether we are the addict, the patient, or the caring partner, there will be adjustments to be made in the relationship. It won't always feel like a celebration from those who sacrificed themselves to walk with us in the difficult seasons if their identity has become enmeshed in our illness. For the one experiencing the miracle, this will be a very difficult concept to grasp.

"Why wouldn't you celebrate me more in my recovery?"

"Why wouldn't you rejoice with me that I'm finally disease free?"

"What is causing this tension simply because I've expressed the need to do things for myself and finally enjoy a life on my terms instead of the terms of my sickness?"

"Why does it press your buttons for me to show up for my own life?"

If we could listen inside the mind of the partner of an addict, the resounding answer to those questions might sound something like this. "Because I'm afraid I won't know who I am if I'm not taking care of you, cleaning up after you literally and figuratively, making excuses for you, or trying to keep some sense of normalcy in what has become a nut house. I have built my entire life around what you need and when you need it. I've been *overly dependable* because you are *completely undependable*. I've become so *predictable* that I bore myself to tears because you are so *unpredictable* that I can't even trust you to get the mail! I have prayed the same prayers over and over so many times that I'm pretty sure I put Jesus to sleep! I'm thrilled that you're disease-free, sober, or whatever the hell you are. But at the end of the day I'm not sure I have the emotional energy left to buy into one more hopeful sober season or spin of the recovery wheel when I have lived in nothing but duty, details, and perpetual disappointment for more years than I care to even count. Frankly, I just don't trust your disease. It isn't even personal. I simply don't trust that I won't be back at square one a year from now and I would rather just bide my time while you have your little candle in the cupcake celebration than risk the emotional devastation that comes with buying in to one more round of hope. So, *yay* for you!

"Now, I need to get to the store."

As cold and lacking empathy as that monologue may sound, some version of that is very often the conversation between an addict and the effected partner after the miracle. The people who have been carrying the mat are tired, fearful, burnt to a crisp, and worn down. Their own faith has been tested for years by the very idea of a God who would even let this happen to them in the first place. While the world around them looks for hope and throws confetti at every sign of an "answer to prayer," the mat carriers learn early on not to order the balloons too soon. Few diseases are as fraught with relapses as addiction and few partners are as emotionally tangled up in their roleplaying as the spouse.

This is what it means to embrace reality in the tension between pain and redemption. To talk about the tension of the miracle—whether it be sobriety, healing of a life-threatening disease, or even the mercy in death after a long season of suffering—sounds like an absurd paradox to many. The reality is that those relational strains take us to places in ourselves we rarely want to admit and they often become resentments waiting to happen for those on both sides of the mat.

Eventually, as we learn to live life apart from our mats, we gradually begin to experience what it means to be fully alive. "Fully alive" is being able to live in the tension of the fully human and fully divine. Fully alive is fully aware and fully awake. It is embracing pain with hope, investing in that which is beyond ourselves to accomplish alone, embracing a way of being that celebrates the journey, packing fewer expectations and making room for anticipation, and freedom from a dualistic mind. We will extend our hand to those who are able to make the journey with us and extend grace to those who, for their own reasons, struggle with us or simply cannot make the journey at all. We will enjoy the gifts of courage and wisdom and eventually serenity on the uncharted road that lies ahead. This is all part of the rocky path home after the miracle.

chapter ten
Do You Want to Be Well?

If someone believes it is our faith that heals us and forgets that it is God who does it, we should ask that person how much faith Lazarus had.

ERIC METAXAS, *MIRACLES.*

*E*ver since I was a small child banging away on my grandmother's piano, I've had a curious confidence that music was going to be my life. Not just a part of my life. My *life*! Music was not merely something I did. It was who I was. Who I am. Music was the little piece of the puzzle that I brought to the world. It was what I was here to give back. I felt God smile on me, just as my grandmother had when I played for her. I like to picture God as Maya Angelou singing along in her rich, tenor voice at my fantasy concert for the great cloud of witnesses.

Music was my prayer without words as if I spoke in the tongues of angels. Melodies were my sanctuary. Creating music has never been just about my talking to God. Music is when I hear God talking back.

Music is the true language of the heart.

I can't recall a single critical life goal or life-choice of mine that didn't involve music. I had always been told I was uniquely gifted and that to steward that gift meant it should be given back to God. In my younger years, what that looked exactly like was up for debate, but somewhere I got the message that it meant performing and writing music God liked.

I eventually realized this gift came with tremendous influence. Music gave me the ability to color the way people perceived things, to alter emotions, and to put the exclamation point on a moment simply by the way I applied my gift.

When I was fifteen, my first song was recorded, and I played on my first recording that same year. By my freshman year in high school, I traveled during the summer months with a Christian music group out of my hometown. In fact, it is the group in which I met my future wife. Tricia was a singer in that same group. For five summers, we roamed the country in a small blue van with shag carpet on the walls. It pulled our gear while a converted horse trailer behind us carried our vinyl LPs.

We looked like the Mystery Machine from Scooby Doo, if, that is, they had been musicians.

At the age of fifteen I wrote what I thought I believed regarding the Christian life, or, at least, what I thought I was supposed to believe. At that young age, I hadn't really reckoned with the duality of my heart. I still believed I was whatever people thought I was. In truth, I was simply the sum of my best-kept secrets.

I was the kid everyone wished they had. I was the shining example. I was the time-honored "good boy" who practiced and did as I was told. I didn't talk back to teachers and was often singled out by them to do special things. I was liked by adults and resented by my peers. I was highly-esteemed by those in authority and I worked overtime to keep it that way. I was lousy at sports and got physically ill at the idea of gym class. My talent plus my persona equaled one very tightly-wound perfectionist in a pre-adolescent body complete with an ulcer. Factor in a culture of Sunday night church, the fear of hell, and a narrow formula for salvation and it becomes easy to understand why I felt as if I had a bomb strapped to my chest most of the time. The bomb being that I might do the unthinkable and actually disappoint someone.

Or worse, God.

The tension's basis was that not only did *I* believe my persona, I also believed I had been entrusted with something valuable and rare. Talent was a privilege, like being born into wealth or having a genius IQ. Talent was something one didn't take lightly and something that could just as easily be taken away at any time if God didn't like the way one was using it (which opened another theological can of worms to sort through later in life). I can't say I believed I was special in a conceited sense, but I did believe I was unique.

Eventually, that uniqueness became a lot to live up to. It became its own persona and it took on an identity all its own. That uniqueness became what author Susan Howatch refers to as our "glittering image." What began as a musically gifted little boy turned into an adult who felt alone and alienated. There was a great price that came with that form of uniqueness. Mostly because it never felt safe to let my guard down or to let people see past the persona and get a glimpse of the real person behind the gift. It didn't feel all that unusual to find myself in situations where I would literally hide from people. As a musician, one gets used to spending hours alone with his or her instrument, so it felt rather normal to be on the outside of what was going on around me.

In all the hiding I tried to do, there was one tiny little glitch, one person I could not hide from: me. Wherever I went, there I was (as the saying goes). I slowly realized my outside didn't match my inside. In fact, I didn't have a category for it. I didn't have a file for a Christian who needed to escape reality so I had to embrace an excuse. My uniqueness gave me that excuse ... and more.

It's a lot of pressure being this special, I reasoned. As I became an adult I began discovering ways to comfort myself that didn't fit the glittering image; I eventually acquired a "get out of jail free" card that I could play. This was the beginning of my private abuse of alcohol and inviting a victim with a sense of entitlement to live in the attic apartment of my psyche.

My religious circles spiritualized and specialized in our glittering images, calling them our *witness*. I had to maintain my *witness*. I wasn't supposed to let anything damage my *witness*. From early on I accepted those narrow ideologies as a spiritual way of saying that I didn't have permission to disappoint anyone or tell anyone the truth about very much. What would people do if they found out I thought this or that, did this or that, saw me in certain places, or said this or that? I couldn't live up to me, much less what other people thought of me so the only option I saw was to begin flying under the radar to find relief.

There began to emerge a second me.

My image. My witness. My persona. The idol of me even I didn't like. My persona showed up to do all the relational and public heavy lifting and I could finally come out from behind it when I knew it was safe, which was when I was alone.

It was no wonder that when I discovered alcohol I thought I'd found the perfect way to medicate my wounded heart and still maintain my glittering image in the world. It worked beautifully! I didn't have to do it out in front of anyone and yet I could have the relief from myself that I needed and believed I deserved. As Kermit the Frog says, "It isn't easy being green." Those of us who are born "green" need to be granted some special dispensations, some wild cards that mere mortals don't need. I needed that "get out of jail free" card because being "green" was killing me.

As I got older I found more and more reasons to use that card. I needed to use it when I wanted to unwind or to "take the edge off." I needed it when I over-served myself and had to have an excuse I could live with. I needed it if I hit more than one red light on the way home from work.

At least that is what I told myself.

I eventually realized that I was living out of a lot of nicely arranged compartments, like neatly stacked emotional luggage. There was the version of *me* that everyone wanted, needed, and bought. There was the more honest inner *me* that really hated that other person. There was the escapist *me* who wanted to disappear and hide in the fog of a good buzz. Then, there was the conflicted *me* who regretted all the above and didn't know how to make sense of any of them. The regretful me tried desperately to integrate all those entities but didn't think they could coexist in one mind. The delusional me even tried to deny that the other versions existed at all. How would it even be possible for all of these personalities to coexist in the heart and mind of a *good Christian*?

The first step I learned is to admit that no one is always a *good Christian*, and that it is okay for that to be true. And while it seems odd to even need to make that point, the fact is my all or nothing perfectionism needed to come to grips with that concept.

I began a long journey of, every day, loading all those people up on a bus and fighting over who got to drive. After my wife's diagnosis, I found myself to be a virtual single parent, nurse, and abandoned spouse. Eventually, the Professional Christian and the caregiver bought seats on the bus as well. Those personas were joining the carpool every day along with all the others who gave their two cents worth every chance they got.

I fast approached a day of reckoning and I knew it. The piper needed to be paid and I had been running up quite a tab. I knew that eventually all the voices sharing the ride would have to be addressed for who and what they really were. Alcohol drove the bus over the edge, but the personas were sitting in the bus, barking out bad directions. With their collective senses of entitlement, skewed perspectives, and shallow views of faith there was no room left for a sane voice anywhere. It would be a long ride filled with angst-ridden trips on that bus before help crested the hill on the horizon for me.

I heard Jesus ask me if I wanted to be well once I saw myself as completely desperate and powerless. If there had been any other way to get help, I would have taken it. "Powerless" and "desperate" weren't words I was used to using when I wrote my resume.

When I finally realized that Jesus was asking me, "Do you want to be well?" in his own figurative way, I really didn't understand it. On the surface, I wanted to quit drinking. In all actuality, I simply wanted to be able to drink like other people. I didn't really want to *stop* drinking. I wanted to be able to stop the way other people stopped at the end of an evening or an event and remain tolerable and married.

I didn't understand what it meant to be truly well at first. I wanted to be well-*ish*. I wanted it on my terms, just without any major surgery. This is when I began the home stretch of my disease that turned into a five-year marathon of daily drinking and a complete takeover by the committee in the crazy bus.

chapter eleven
Prayers and Promises

Let's not be afraid to look at everything that has brought us to where we are now and trust that we will soon see in it the guiding hand of a loving God.

HENRI NOUWEN, *BREAD FOR THE JOURNEY*

What do we do when we find that we have been trying to square certain faith perspectives against life's realities only to find that they don't fit? Why is it that when push comes to shove our human nature is to use our faith system as a means by which we try to manipulate God, circumstances, or other people? How do we learn to distinguish sincere prayer from evangelical superstition? Where do we run when God doesn't just zap us sober, or healed, or remove all the tension from our difficult marriages and relationships? How can we incorporate our new life of rigorous honesty into a life that includes being rigorously honest with God? I believe that one of the best places to start is to examine the way we approach the concept of prayer.

If God had struck me sober the way I asked him to in my early attempts at sobriety it would have robbed me of everything this new way of life has become for me over the last decade. It isn't about *not* drinking. It never *was* about the drinking. The drinking was the messy part, the part that was going to get me into deeper and deeper trouble, and maybe even kill me. Alcohol was my favorite solution that quit working, as they say. But alcohol wasn't my ultimate problem. My problem, among many problems, was that I was using prayer to preach to God instead of listening. My confessions were shrouded in veiled obscure language that never specifically owned the true pain that I inflicted on others or experienced myself. I had long embraced evangelical superstitions that led me into a performance based relationship with a God who wanted to be flattered instead of honestly worshipped for all his mystery. I couldn't square how I could be powerless over something when my faith preached that I was supposed to be able "to do all things through Christ who strengthened me," which left me confused, frustrated, and angry. Making promises and mustering up what I thought was sincerity was the only way I knew to make amends with God and the people I constantly disappointed.

Praying was an exercise that exhausted me because it better resembled leaving God a string of long voicemails and hanging up. "Hey God, it's me again. I'm doing okay. Here's what's going on. I assume you need to hear me say it out loud so here goes..."

One of the first principles I learned in recovery was that my only hope for freedom required that I learn to accept life on life's terms. We can't change people, places, or things. Many of us have made a lifelong pursuit out of trying to get the rest of the world to march to the beat of our drum only to find that they weren't all that interested in keeping in step. Instead of surrendering those people and situations to the care of God, we dug in deeper. After the miracle, we realized that by praying for God to only change our circumstances (or other people), we had deflected the denial that was rooted in our own hearts. Most of us approached prayer as more of an experience that we could walk away from hoping to feel a little more confident, a little more comfortable, and maybe just a tiny bit happier than we were before.

Before our miracle, many of us avoided the prayers of people who brought their candid questions and doubts to God, those who were suffering losses, living with chronic and terminal illness, watching their children self-destruct, or just plain wearing themselves out in the name of Jesus. Their prayers made us fidget and twitch as we listened to their raw confessions and questions. Maybe we were uncomfortable because somewhere deep down we thought, "If I can avoid their doubts and realities, then I don't have to confront my own." After the miracle, we realized that we were those people and we had doubts, questions, and pain of our own.

I remember being with a group of friends who were praying for the disintegrating marriage of a couple we all knew. The overriding theme of the group's petition to God was that he needed to intervene and do a miracle in the hearts of this couple. "Just give them a fresh love for one another. Help them see that to break up this family would be a mistake."

Ultimately and predictably, someone played the "God hates divorce" card, as if to read from the statutes of all that makes a marriage legally binding placing God on the bench of divorce court. After listening to everyone preach to God for quite a while on behalf of this poor, estranged couple I became uncomfortable but managed to keep my opinions to myself ... for the moment.

Later, I told a friend who was present that I was astonished at how simplistic we were being about the pain and specific issues complicating the lives of this family. My friend asked me to elaborate.

"No one in that circle asked God to reveal to the couple the damaging behaviors and cycles that they had learned," I answered. "For instance, why is it that no one asked God to bring counsel into their lives that addressed the way they had each adopted a victimized persona that allowed them to hold on to their resentments perpetuating a sense of entitlement which they were both using to justify their hurtful behavior to one another?"

My friend looked rather puzzled. "But our job is to pray that they stay together and that God heal their marriage," he said.

"No! Their marriage isn't the *point*. God wants to heal them as individuals regardless of whether the marriage can survive or not. If they don't address these core personal issues they will just take them into their next marriage. The marriage is just a big red flag telling you what is going on in their individual pain. Praying that God just gives them emotional amnesia and they wake up gaga over one another again tomorrow does nothing. Praying for them to just play nicely together and like each other for the sake of the kids is like asking a drowning person to pretend they are swimming the backstroke to Cuba."

Needless to say, I am not invited to be on the prayer chain at my church ... which may be a good thing.

Let me hasten to add that I believe in saving marriages, praying for marriages and families, and I believe that God hates divorce as much as he hates the pain that brings us to it. However, it seems to me that if one or both parties can't own the patterns that are killing them, their partner, or their marriage, then Jesus will weep with you all the way to the courthouse and hold your purse while you file the papers. Lest we get too bogged down here on our respective positions regarding divorce, I want to take us back to the point of prayer. At the end of the day, most of us find ourselves focused on our circumstances and asking God to change them rather than asking for the core issues of our hearts to be addressed and challenged.

For some who come from certain doctrinal perspectives praying the *right* way with the *right* faith in the *right* atmosphere theoretically yields the desired results. For them, prayer is *all* about results. This is when the idea of prayer appeals to our need to feel in control (which always arouses our old ways of thinking and being). Those who believe that they simply need to get enough people praying for a certain outcome to sway the vote in heaven can either find themselves devastatingly disappointed, or even more determined to work harder next time to garner support. Prayer comes off being used like a cosmic petition—with enough signatures, God will be convinced to change his position on a circumstance and grant the desired result. After all, isn't God *always* persuaded by how he's doing in the polls?

These are also the same voices that console us with the adage that God won't allow us more than we can bear. If there is one piece of Christian folklore I would like to crucify it is this cliché that we throw around so that we don't have to experience the truest depth of someone else's despair or our deepest fear. This nugget of wisdom is nowhere in the Bible. It may be a paraphrase regarding temptation from 1 Corinthians, but I'll leave that to the theologians to determine.

God is *constantly* allowing us more than we can bear. That is why prayer after the miracle looks more like people coming together to surrender themselves and their circumstances to the will of God and seek the courage to accept it. We must believe that even in this unbearable grief, loss, or illness he is holding us in his arms. Courage, peace, and wisdom are the three things I believe God *actually* promises to grant us in our suffering before *and* after the miracle. This is the path of serenity and the beginning of wisdom.

At times, we treat prayer as though we believe God uses it to weigh our sincerity so he can decide how he will dispense our ultimate consequences. The more we can use prayer to demonstrate our sincerity to God, the more likely we are to convince him we are deserving of our desired outcome. This is usually accompanied by a lot of promise making and bargaining with God, which is another favorite that those of us who found ourselves powerless over our circumstances have dabbled in. Somewhere in the evolution of our story we developed a concept of repentance that required blanket promises, contracts, and vows.

What we discover after the miracle is that it wasn't our promises or our bargaining that brought about our freedom. In fact, those things *kept* us sick because those were all part of the hamster wheel of performance that drained our souls dry.

One of the biggest reliefs for me in my healing process was when I realized I didn't need to promise God, my family, or anyone else anything at all. What I *could* say was that I wanted to live my life one moment at a time knowing God was already fully satisfied with me. Enough of those days strung together would be called sobriety.

There were, of course those days that I didn't want to, or that I only wanted to want to but even the hardest days didn't mean I had to resort to saying what I thought God wanted to hear for me to find peace.

There is a prayer by the mystic, Thomas Merton that I love and pray often, especially when I'm not sure how to pray. That prayer is this: "My Lord God, I have no idea where I am going. I do not see the road ahead of me. I cannot know for certain where it will end. Nor do I really know myself, and the fact that I think that I am following your will does not mean that I am actually doing so. But I believe that the desire to please you does in fact please you. And I hope I have that desire in all that I am doing. I hope that I will never do anything apart from that desire. And I know that if I do this you will lead me by the right road though I may know nothing about it. Therefore will I trust you always though I may seem to be lost and in the shadow of death. I will not fear, for you are ever with me, and you will never leave me to face my perils alone." [3]

This was not a prayer that I could pray before the miracle because I needed certainty and results. Waiting on the Lord is something I'm learning a little more about than I ever cared to know, quite honestly. It is one thing to say I belong to Jesus and I have a certain hope as a Christian. It is quite another to say I am willing to let go of my excuses and facades, strip myself of all my favorite substitutes, and lay myself bare—poor before Him, as Brennan Manning says, and simply wait. I'm finding that peace can reside in the fear as well as the freedom. And waiting on the Lord is simply waiting—quietly, patiently, and purposefully as we acknowledge all our human limitations. This is *living* prayer. It is the kind of prayer that sustains us and reminds us of who we are and who God is because we tend to quickly forget.

---

3   Thomas Merton, *Thoughts in Solitude* (New York: Farrar, Straus & Cudahy, 1958)

chapter twelve
The Miracle of Desperation

*There is a beautiful transparency to honest
disciples who never wear a false face and do not
pretend to be anything but who they are*

BRENNAN MANNING

For most of us, entering sobriety was like wandering into a desert. At times, it felt as if there wasn't another living soul around for miles. Maybe it is because admitting powerlessness and embracing the miracle of desperation brings such a sense of wandering into an isolated wasteland. Who would voluntarily experience that? The phrase sounds like such a gross contradiction, doesn't it—the miracle of desperation? After all, most miracles are thought to deliver us *from* the wilderness, not *into* it. I feel much more of an empathetic posture toward the Israelites who longed for the familiarity of Egypt after so many years of wandering. At least Egypt was predictable. And the biblical story tells us that many would have returned to it (relapsed) if they had been given the opportunity. Rethinking our recovery is nothing new. It has been around sense the twelve tribes and most likely before that.

In his novel *The Garden of Eden,* Ernest Hemingway writes, "You'll ache. And you're going to love it. It will crush you. And you're still going to love it. Doesn't it sound lovely beyond belief?" Regardless of one's opinion of Hemingway or his androgynous novel, the quote stands as a brutally honest testimony to what it means to feel again, to find our voice in the valley, and to live in the tension of pain and freedom. The book summarizes our journey into our next chapter after the door locks behind us and we realize we can't go back. This is the exhilarating moment when we grasp the concept that the only way through it is *through it*. In that moment, to believe that we will be whole on the other side of that experience is asking a lot.

The irony of the desert walk—and what no one seemed to remember to tell us—is that this is not a journey to be feared, but celebrated. This healthy trepidation, this hopeful distress, is exactly how we need to feel in this particular frame of the big picture. Heroic sobriety is an oxymoron. And yet those of us entering early recovery have some false notion that everyone else who has traveled the road before us was "just an alcoholic" who suddenly got sober and became Joan of Arc. As if we were "just

Clark Kent" with a hangover waiting for our first twelve-step meeting so we could break out the red cape.

The truth is that there has never been one addict who let go of their security blanket of choice without fear and trembling. Most people believe that fear to be the idea of letting go of a substance or behavior. The true fear, in fact, is that we will now have to face our feelings, emotions, and conflicts without anesthesia ... and that is more terrifying than letting go of a substance or behavior.

Up to this point we have been dead to our feelings, paralyzed at the belief that we could have a voice in our own lives, and most of all numbed out to our own reality and truth. We have been in crisis mode and damage control for so long, we haven't even had the luxury of feeling angry about how we got here. I say luxury because, if we think about it, anger is a bit of a luxurious emotion. Most of the time we only get to experience it *after* the crisis, assuming we make it that far. In the midst *of* the crisis, fight or flight consumes the moments. Our minds are a squirrel cage of reactions and overthinking, allowing little opportunity or capacity to explore how we genuinely feel about any of our negative repercussions and consequences. Suddenly, as we were sleepwalking through our own lives and our addictions, desperation had the audacity to jar us from our sleep. We took our first steps into the vast unknown called healing and we found ourselves once again, alone with our own emotions—emotions which most especially included our anger.

For many of us, anger had previously been an unsafe emotion. Some even associate it with sin or displeasing God. But I believe that anger, aimed in the right direction, can create a righteous motivation that causes us to abandon any notion of going back to our old way of being.

I often have my clients write a letter addressed to "Shame" as if it is a criminal awaiting sentencing while we, the victims, get the opportunity to read our letter before the judge and let Shame know just how utterly outraged we are at everything it robbed us of when we bought in to its deceitful message. I urge people to get as angry as they need to be at their shame and fire away using both barrels. For most addicts shame is a major trigger in addiction and the first stop to a relapse if we don't address it. Many find this helpful, and by addressing the thief of hearts on *this* side of the miracle, they discover their voice as they set out on the path to forgiving themselves.

While we may be tempted to compromise, minimize, or marginalize our needs, emotions, and reality, our desperation simply will not let us. The desert has called out the thirst in us, which has always been there and has given us the strength to give it a name. This is often the season when we finally give ourselves permission to explore what we truly need our new life to look like, what we need from those around us, and what we need from ourselves. As we embrace the reality of our true emotions and give voice to them, we realize that this moment is the official beginning of our new normal.

We emerge from this walk in the wilderness with much less self-consciousness and a much greater sense of purpose and confidence. We know that we have done important work and we have been granted the rare gift of experiencing God in tangible ways. We have heard the Spirit singing over us in the winds of the dusty landscape and His song is what will sustain us as we reclaim and rename what is left of our lives.

For our loved ones who have had to wait for us at the edge of this crossing, it has been an agonizing exercise in trust. Who will be the person that emerges from this passage? Will there be a relationship left to salvage? Will the miracle of sobriety and the healing of the addict interrupt the reality of the awaiting loved one to the point that they will also make their own journey into healing?

These answers will be as unique as the individuals who experience the questions, but the possibility of promise is the same for everyone. Embracing the desperation will give us more courage than fear to ask ourselves the hard questions about where we will go from here. This is where our pain will be greater than our fear of change. Pain is always the great motivator in our moving forward. Remember, the door locked *behind* us, so the only *normal* we will experience from here is the new one we must create.

For those of us with spouses and partners we will "do" life in a face-to-face way that will call on us to name the true conflicts in our relationships. We are removing our common enemy of substances, compulsive behavior, and addiction and we will soon be faced with the reality of who we really are together as a couple and a family. Losing our common enemy of addiction, substances, and compulsivity is going to leave a vacuum that may either be filled with blame and suspicion, or grace and calling one another into honest conversation. Fear and blame-shifting will be a temptation, but our new understanding of shame will allow us to stare it down and remember who we really are from here. As recovering people, we will no longer volunteer to take on the assigned blame we once did when we believed that *we* were the only problem in the relationship. The clarity that comes with our walk through desperation will equip us to take our proper place in the conversation.

When we emerge from the miracle we will see the roles that others around us have played for what they truly are. We will learn to be quick to correct the enabler, lovingly silence the persecutor, and seek the wisdom God promises in our new paradigm. As I have stressed many times in this book, our loved ones will be challenged by our new way of being. We have to understand that we answered *yes* to the call to be well but those around us may have had other ideas about what a healthy version of us will feel like. They may pray for the idea of a healthy spouse, but resent the fresh opinions, evolving spirituality, and upside-down view of the world that comes with it. There is no single answer for this relational perplexity. Each situation will have its own unique dynamics and what will happen in each scenario will vary from case to case.

It is important to note that if you must stop being *you* so that someone else can stay *them* we have a huge problem. Many in early recovery feel that the tension in the home which comes with early sobriety is their fault and they question the personal progress they've made individuating from their marriage if it causes any conflict or consternation for the spouse. The presence of conflict doesn't mean that there is blame to be placed on either partner. It simply means that the relational playing field is plowed up and everyone is learning a new game. Fresh sobriety and relationships are fraught with this specific conflict more often than not. This is why family work is so important in the recovery process and why I stress working with the family members of all my substance abuse clients.

This relational dissension is not exclusive to spouses and partners but can also be true of employers, siblings, children, and anyone who holds deep relational equity in our lives. The process of exerting ourselves is the same regardless. It is reasonable on their part to expect us to go about rebuilding trust and demonstrating a very humble point of view as we re-enter their world. However, whether it is addiction, an affair, a death, or anything that has upset the relational applecart, we have to remind ourselves over and over that the old normal is gone. In order to thrive from here we must be able to address our truest needs and model what our new role in the relationship is going to be. We have to retrain the people around us in the same way we have had to retrain ourselves. If we resort to performing in our old role in the relationship just to make an insecure partner feel safe instead of respecting our new boundaries and addressing our needs, it is only a matter of time until we will relapse into our old way of acting and thinking, which will almost inevitably result in a relapse of our abuse disorder. It is imperative to continue to think soberly as well as live soberly. Every relapse starts in our thinking and our behavior, not when we pick up our first drink after rehab.

As we come forth from the wilderness of our desperation, we should keep some sand in our sandals to remind us of where we've been. I write a blog *The Rock in My Shoe* (http://davidbhampton.com/blog/). I chose that title because I write about where I've been and the reminders that God has left me with from my journey.

I even name the rocks that have remained in my shoe so I am reminded of the walks through the wastelands. The rocks can be painful, but they can also be tiny fragments that remind me of God's faithfulness to me regardless of who has been able to go the distance with me on my journey. The jagged pebbles in my shoe keep me aware of my need to seek God's voice along the path. They allow me to celebrate where I've been instead of bemoaning those paths. They tell me that my story is sacred and that even the insanity has a place because it brought me to who I truly am.

We don't get that without the miracle of desperation.

So, take up your bed and walk. You're forgiven. Now forgive yourself. Address the true enemies in your life: shame, fear, and the accusing voices from the committee in your head. Make your peace with shame. Redirect your anger. Buy a timeshare at the intersection of Desperation and Gratitude and experience true worship. Ask for what you need in your relationships and give others the opportunity to be who they *can* be in the situation. Give them the opportunity to know the truest version of you. You will reap the joy of being known. If that isn't something that your loved one can embrace then you will soon realize that you can only have relationship to the extent that they can accept the most transparent version of who you are, not the extent to which you must earn it from them by performing. These are but a few of the small steps into freedom after the miracle.

Remember, you have been saved! This is the greatest miracle of all. But even redemption has its challenges. Step into the desert places and let God speak. Emerge and speak your truth. This is healing. This is restoration. This is salvation.

So, the question remains: *Do you want to be well?*

about the author

*D*avid Hampton has lived in Nashville, TN since 1988. His experiences include two stints as a staff songwriter for major music publishers, touring as a musician with various Christian music artists, and most recently as the author of a book, Our Authentic Selves: Reflections On What We Believe and What We Wish We Believed (Lighthouse Publishing).

David served in the position of Director of Worship and Arts Ministries at Christ Community Church in Franklin,

TN since 1995. After the death of his wife, Tricia, in May of 2013 from complications due to multiple sclerosis, David began exploring a new career path pursuing certification as a nationally accredited addiction recovery professional. After completing his certification process he left his longtime position at Christ Community in August of 2016 to devote himself fulltime to his private practice as a Certified Professional Addiction/Recovery Coach as part of a counseling group in Brentwood, TN.

As a man with his own personal story of addiction and recovery he is also cofounder of Entreat Recovery Partners; a nonprofit group helping connect those who struggle with addiction and substance use disorder to medically assisted treatment, trauma and Adverse Childhood Experience therapy, 12 step communities, as well as coaching for cognitive restructuring. This multifaceted approach to recovery care is becoming widely accepted as a best practices treatment modality the more we recognize addiction as a multi-faceted disorder.

As a public speaker, David shares his story of recovery and restoration with various groups and organizations around the country hoping to help bridge the gap of understanding between faith communities and the world of addiction recovery.

David continues to enjoy various musical opportunities in Nashville as well as writing, traveling, and speaking.

To book David for your next conference, retreat, fundraiser, or event contact Ambassador Speakers at ambassadorspeakers.com.

To keep up with David's upcoming events, new materials, and blog go to davidbhampton.com.

Morgan James
Speakers Group

www.TheMorganJamesSpeakersGroup.com

We connect Morgan James published
authors with live and online events
and audiences who will benefit
from their expertise.

Printed in the USA
CPSIA information can be obtained
at www.ICGtesting.com
JSHW021357220424
61664JS00005B/326

9 781683 505778